my revision notes

AQA A-level

RELIGIOUS STUDIES:
PAPER 2 STUDY OF CHRISTIANITY AND DIALOGUES

Sheila Butler

HODDER
EDUCATION
AN HACHETTE UK COMPANY

The Publishers would like to thank the following for permission to reproduce copyright material.

Acknowledgements

All extracts quoted from the Bible throughout have been taken from the New International Version.

Every effort has been made to trace all copyright holders, but if any have been inadvertently overlooked, the Publishers will be pleased to make the necessary arrangements at the first opportunity.

Although every effort has been made to ensure that website addresses are correct at time of going to press, Hodder Education cannot be held responsible for the content of any website mentioned in this book. It is sometimes possible to find a relocated web page by typing in the address of the home page for a website in the URL window of your browser.

Hachette UK's policy is to use papers that are natural, renewable and recyclable products and made from wood grown in sustainable forests. The logging and manufacturing processes are expected to conform to the environmental regulations of the country of origin.

Orders: please contact Bookpoint Ltd, 130 Park Drive, Milton Park, Abingdon, Oxon OX14 4SE. Telephone: (44) 01235 827720. Fax: (44) 01235 400401. Email education@ bookpoint.co.uk Lines are open from 9 a.m. to 5 p.m., Monday to Saturday, with a 24-hour message answering service. You can also order through our website: www. hoddereducation.co.uk

ISBN: 9781510425880

First published in 2018 by
Hodder Education,
An Hachette UK Company
Carmelite House
50 Victoria Embankment
London EC4Y 0DZ

www.hoddereducation.co.uk

Impression number   10 9 8 7 6 5 4 3 2

Year   2022 2021 2020 2019 2018

Cover photo © Vandathai/Shutterstock.com
Illustrations by Integra
Typeset in India by Integra
Printed in India

A catalogue record for this title is available from the British Library.

Get the most from this book

These revision notes will help you to revise for AQA A-level Religious Studies: Paper 2 Study of Religion and Dialogues, or AQA AS-level Religious Studies: Paper 2 Study of Religion. Everyone has to decide his or her own revision strategy, but it is essential to review your work, learn it and test your understanding.

These revision notes will help you to do that in a planned way, topic by topic. This books aims to give you the essentials that should serve as a reminder of what you will have covered in your course and allow you to bring together your own learning and understanding.

It is essential to review your work, learn it and test your understanding. Tick each box in the contents page when you have:
● revised and understood a topic
● checked your understanding
● practised the exam questions.

You can also keep track of your revision by ticking off each topic heading in the book. You may find it helpful to add your own notes as you work through each topic.

Features to help you succeed

Key terms
Clear, concise definitions of essential key terms are provided where they first appear.

Key quotations
It is crucial that you can write about religious teachings in your exam. Almost all the questions demand this. This book includes many teachings to use, but you should look to add your own too.

Now test yourself
These short, knowledge-based questions provide the first step in testing your learning. Answers are available online.

Exam practice
Practice exam questions are provided for each topic. Use them to consolidate your revision and practise your exam skills.

Exam tips
Expert tips are given to help you polish your exam technique in order to maximise your chances in the exam.

Typical mistake
The author identifies some typical mistakes candidates make and explains how you can avoid them.

Online
Go online to see answers to the Now Test Yourself questions, and find examiner-commentaries on sample Exam Practice questions, which will help you to assess your answers. You will find these at **www.hoddereducation.co.uk/myrevisionnotes**

My revision planner

REVISED   TESTED   EXAM READY

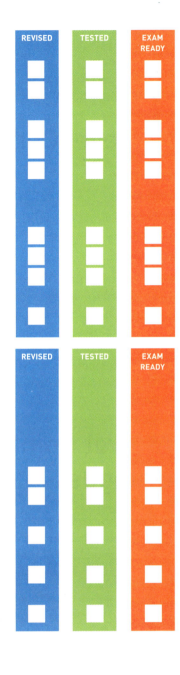

Introduction

You can use these revision notes to revise for AS- or A-level Religious Studies for AQA. Your qualification is made up of two components:
- Component 1: Philosophy of religion and ethics
- Component 2: Study of religion and dialogues (A-level), or Study of religion (AS-level).

These revision notes cover only Component 2. You can use My Revision Notes AQA A-level Religious Studies: Paper 1 Philosophy of religion and ethics to revise for Component 1.

AS-level Component 2: Study of religion

Content

For Component 2, you will have studied one of five of the world's major religions: Buddhism, Christianity, Hinduism, Islam or Judaism.

These revision notes will help you to revise if you studied Christianity. Within Christianity, you will have studied the following topics:
- Sources of wisdom and authority
- God
- Self, death and afterlife
- Good conduct and key moral principles
- Expressions of religious identity.

How the Assessment works

Component 2 is examined by one written exam, which is 1 hour long.

This paper consists of two compulsory two-part questions.
- The first part of each question tests AO1 and is worth 15 marks.
- The second part of each question tests AO2 and is worth 15 marks.
- So the total maximum mark for the whole paper is 60 marks.

This component represents 33 per cent of your overall AS-level.

A-level Component 2: Study of religion and dialogues

Content

For Component 2, you will have studied one of five of the world's major religions: Buddhism, Christianity, Hinduism, Islam or Judaism.

These revision notes will help you to revise if you studied Christianity. Within Christianity, you will have studied the following topics:
- Sources of wisdom and authority
- God
- Self, death and afterlife
- Good conduct and key moral principles
- Expressions of religious identity
- Christianity, gender and sexuality
- Christianity and science
- Christianity and the challenge of secularisation
- Christianity, migration and religious pluralism.

How the Assessment works

Component 2 is examined by one written exam, which is 3 hours long. This paper is split into three sections.

The total maximum mark for the whole paper is 100 marks.

Section A: Study of Christianity

This section contains two compulsory two-part questions.
- The first part of each question tests AO1 and is worth 10 marks.
- The second part of each question tests AO2 and is worth 15 marks.
- So the total maximum mark for this section of the paper is 50 marks.

Section B: The dialogue between philosophy of religion and Christianity
- You have to answer one unstructured synoptic question from a choice of two.
- This question is worth 25 marks.

Section C: The dialogue between ethics and Christianity
- You have to answer one unstructured synoptic question from a choice of two.
- This question is worth 25 marks.

This component represents 50 per cent of your overall A-level.

Now test yourself answers at www.hoddereducation.co.uk/myrevisionnotes

Preparing for the examinations

Remember that two skills are assessed in the exam, but there are some general points that apply to both parts of each question.

- Ensure that your writing is legible. Examiners cannot mark or give credit for what they cannot read.
- Spend a minute or two in jotting down a very brief plan (words and phrases, not sentences) of relevant points that you might include.
- Remain focused on the question throughout. Answer the question that is set, not the one that you would like it to be.
- Include reference to scholarly opinion, whether a school of thought or a named scholar, but do not confuse them.
- Use specialist terms and spell them correctly.
- Paragraph your work. Use a new paragraph for each of your main ideas or arguments.

AO1 is assessed in the first part of each of the two questions

- The command word for AS-level is 'explain'.
- The command word for A-level is 'examine'.
- AO1 tests knowledge and understanding. Your answer to the first part of each question should not contain any evaluation.
- Do not give a general introduction stating your intent by repeating the question or setting out what you intend to cover in your answer. That is a waste of valuable time.
- Give a range of points in your answer but do not try to include so many that your answer becomes like a list because you do not have time for development.
- Develop each of the points you make with further comment and support them with evidence, including, as appropriate, reference to scripture.
- Be aware of chronology. Do not, for instance, state that Aquinas disagreed with embryo research.
- Aim at fulfilling the Level 5 criteria, as shown in the table below.

AS-level (13–15 marks)	A-level (9–10 marks)
<ul><li>Knowledge and understanding is accurate and relevant and is consistently applied to the question.</li><li>Very good use of detailed and relevant evidence which may include textual/scriptural references where appropriate.</li><li>The answer is clear and coherent and there is effective use of specialist language and terminology.</li></ul>	<ul><li>Knowledge and critical understanding is accurate, relevant and fully developed in breadth and depth with very good use of detailed and relevant evidence which may include textual/scriptural references where appropriate.</li><li>Where appropriate, good knowledge and understanding of the diversity of views and/or scholarly opinion is demonstrated.</li><li>Clear and coherent presentation of ideas with precise use of the appropriate subject vocabulary.</li></ul>

AO2 is assessed in the second part of each question

- The structure of the question for AS-level consists of a statement followed by the command 'Assess this view'.
- The structure of the question for A-level consists of a statement followed by the command 'Evaluate this claim'.
- This tests your ability to analyse arguments or viewpoints and to evaluate them.
- AO2 is not about giving one set of views, then another set of views and finally giving your own view. Such a response would consist mainly of AO1. It is about assessing the persuasiveness and reasonableness of an argument by examining the strengths of its claims and the strengths of the counter-arguments.
- First of all, set out clearly and coherently the argument in support of this claim.
- Then give critical analysis of the argument. This might involve raising some of the following questions about the argument:
  - Is it inconsistent or illogical at any point?
  - Does it make any unjustified assumptions?
  - Does it give reasonable evidence in support of its claims or does it ignore or downplay evidence that might count against the argument or alternative interpretations of the evidence?
  - Does it exaggerate its claims or make sweeping generalisations?
  - Does it include subjective and biased opinion?
- Use trigger words such as 'however', 'additionally' or 'nevertheless' to help the examiner see where you are making critical analysis.
- This should lead you to include consideration of at least one different viewpoint from the argument in support of the statement.
  - There is no need to consider more than two different viewpoints in your answer.
  - They need not be opposing viewpoints.
- This should lead you finally to an evaluation of the argument, i.e. to an assessment of its value.
  - You might assess it as convincing.
  - You might think it fails because of the flaws it contains or because a different argument or viewpoint is more persuasive.
  - You might conclude that it is difficult to come to a definitive conclusion.
- At the very start of your answer note any key terms or phrases in the statement and ensure that you address them throughout your answer; this will ensure a fully focused response.
- Aim at fulfilling the Level 5 criteria, as shown in the table.

AS-level (13–15 marks)	A-level (13–15 marks)
<ul><li>Reasoned and evidenced chains of reasoning supporting different points of view with critical analysis.</li><li>Evaluation is based on the reasoning presented.</li><li>The answer is clear and coherent and there is effective use of specialist language and terminology.</li></ul>	<ul><li>A very well-focused response to the issue(s) raised.</li><li>Perceptive discussion of different views, including, where appropriate, those of scholars or schools of thought with critical analysis.</li><li>There is an appropriate evaluation fully supported by the reasoning.</li><li>Precise use of the appropriate subject vocabulary.</li></ul>

1 Sources of wisdom and authority

Introduction to the Bible

What is the Bible?

REVISED

- The word 'Bible' means 'books' and it is Christianity's sacred text.
- It is a collection of books that express beliefs about God and God's purposes for humanity and the rest of the created world.
- The earliest writings date from early in the first millennium BCE, but some are based on oral traditions that are many centuries older.
- The latest writings belong to the second century CE.
- The Bible falls into two parts: the Old Testament and the New Testament.
- The books of the Old and New Testaments together form the **Canon of the Bible**.

The Old Testament

- The **Old Testament** contains the writings of the Jewish scriptures (the *Tenakh*) though the order is different.
- It was in fixed form by the first century BCE.
- Some of the writing is in prose but much is in poetry; it contains a wide range of different types of literature.
- There are four main parts:
  - The first five books are known as the Torah ('law') and they do contain many law codes, e.g. the Ten Commandments, but they tell the history of the origins of the Jews, starting with the creation of the universe and ending with the death of Moses.
  - Historical writings that tell the history of the Jews from the conquest of Canaan and ending in the period of Persian rule in the fifth century BCE.
  - The prophetic books contain the insights of individuals into God's purposes for Israel.
  - Wisdom literature covers a wide range of themes and types of writing. It includes an examination of the suffering of the innocent, erotic love poetry and a commentary on life that is at times cynical and agnostic.

The New Testament

- The **New Testament** contains Christian writings that date mainly from the first century.
- It reached fixed form by the fourth century CE.
- There are four main parts:
  - The Gospels contain the good news about Jesus, recounting his ministry, passion (suffering and death) and resurrection.
  - The Acts of the Apostles is a history of the early Church.
  - The Epistles are letters written mainly to Christian communities to give guidance on belief and lifestyle.
  - The Book of Revelation uses graphic imagery to describe the Last Judgement.

> **Testament** means 'covenant'/'agreement'.
>
> **Canon of the Bible** refers to those books believed by the leaders of the early Christian Church to be inspired by God and therefore authoritative.
>
> **Old Testament** refers to the covenant that God made with Israel on Mt Sinai through Moses.
>
> **New Testament** refers to the covenant made by God with humanity through the death of Jesus.

Now test yourself

1 What beliefs overall do the books of the Bible contain?
2 What is the meaning of the word 'Testament'?
3 What are the four main parts of the Old Testament?
4 What are the four main parts of the New Testament?
5 What is meant by the phrase 'the Canon of the Bible'?

TESTED

The nature and authority of the Bible

Conservative approaches

Evangelical Protestants

Many evangelical Protestants hold whvat is called a fundamentalist view of the nature and authority of the Bible. They believe:

- The Bible is the infallible word of God; it contains no mistakes of any kind.
- The authors were directly inspired by God.
- Apparent contradictions in content are due to the limitations of the human intellect, i.e. they are not real contradictions.
- When it comes to the Genesis story of creation, there are different approaches among fundamentalists, but all agree that the account given is true.
  - Those known as young earth creationists have a literalist approach to the Bible and reject any theories that contradict the literal meaning of Genesis 1.
  - Those known as old earth creationists regard Genesis 1 as giving a scientifically correct account of the origins of the universe; they do not adopt a literalist approach.

> **Exam tip**
>
> There are many differing views on the nature and authority of the Bible among Christians and the labels attached to each of these views vary. What actual label you use does not matter as much as your ability to show that you understand the differences in understanding among Christians.

> **Key quotation**
>
> All Scripture is God-breathed and is useful for teaching, rebuking, correcting and training in righteousness.
>
> 2 Timothy 3:16

Two fundamentalist approaches to Genesis 1	
Young earth creationist	Old earth creationist
• Creation occurred about 6,000 years ago (using Bible genealogies) • Literalist understanding of the text • Creation in six days means literally six days • Creation of every species is a separate act of creation • Humans essentially different from animals • Scientific theories rejected as products of limited and mistaken human intelligence • Some say that fossil evidence was planted by God to make the earth look old and test faith	• Acceptance of scientific dating of universe, i.e. circa 13.8 billion years ago • Not literalist, e.g. Hebrew word for day has more than one meaning • Creation in six epochs/stages • Acceptance within limits of Darwinian evolution • Humans a 'special' creation, i.e. different from animals • Genesis 1 and modern science compatible, e.g. 'let there be light' refers to the Big Bang and the six 'days' match the six stages of the evolution of the cosmos according to scientific thinking

Catholic views

- The Bible is inspired by God, but was written by human beings.
- The inspiration, i.e. the way in which it is the word of God, relates to the Bible as a whole rather than to each word or verse.
- They distinguish between the key messages in the Bible regarding salvation, which they believe are without error, and the accounts of the individual authors who were products of their time and culture, and need to be understood in that context.
- Genesis 1 was never intended as a scientific or factual account of the origins of the universe; the author used the genre of myth to convey truths about the nature of God as creator and the nature of humanity and of the created world.

- Guidance in interpreting the Bible comes from **Tradition** and the **Magisterium**, as well as the use of the individual's informed conscience and reason.

> **Key quotation**
>
> The Bible is not meant to convey precise historical information or scientific findings to us. Moreover, the authors were children of their time. Their forms of expression are influenced by the sometimes inadequate cultural images of the world around them. Nevertheless, everything that man must know about God and the way of his salvation is found with infallible certainty in Sacred Scripture.
>
> *Dei Verbum*

> **Tradition** refers to teachings, customs and practices of the Church passed down through the centuries and seen as equal in importance to the Bible.
>
> **Magisterium** refers to the teaching authority of the Pope and bishops who preserve and interpret the Bible and Tradition.

Neo-orthodox approaches

REVISED

Neo-orthodox approaches are based on the arguments of philosophers like Karl Barth.

Karl Barth (1886–1968)

Karl Barth was a Swiss Protestant theologian who believed that the Bible:
- is not the word of God but it contains the word of God
- is the way through which humans may experience God, realising their need for forgiveness and divine mercy shown through Jesus
- is not inerrant with respect to science, history and religion, as its writers were products of their time and subject to limitations of intellect.

Liberal approaches

REVISED

This term covers a wide range of approaches:
- Some believe that those who wrote the texts were guided by God.
- Others believe that the Bible is an entirely human document, consisting of what the writers believed about God and his purposes for the world.
- What individual authors wrote was a product of the culture and age in which each of them lived and of their particular temperament and outlook on life.
- The Bible is not inspired, but it may be inspiring to individuals, e.g. Jesus' statement in Matthew 26:52 that those who draw the sword will die by the sword may inspire some Christians to adopt a pacifist approach to war.
- The Sea of Faith Network, which includes Christians with very liberal views, claims that faith is a purely human creation, so the Bible has no authority other than any that an individual might choose to give it.

> **Now test yourself**
>
> TESTED
>
> 1 How is the Catholic view of the Bible as the word of God different from that of Evangelical Protestants?
> 2 What is the key difference between young earth and old earth creationist approaches to Genesis 1?
> 3 What did Karl Barth say about the Bible as the word of God?
> 4 Give three ways in which liberal Christians understand the nature of the Bible.

The authority of the Church

Outline history of the Church

- After his resurrection Jesus gave the **Apostles** authority to lead the Church.
- The Apostles passed on their authority to new leaders (**bishops**) and this transmission of authority continued down the centuries.
- It became known as the **Apostolic Succession**.
- In Western Europe, the Bishop of Rome (known as the **Pope**) was the leader of the Church and everyone had to obey him.
- In the sixteenth century, many Christians rebelled against the Pope's authority and they became known as Protestants (because they protested against the established Church).
- From the sixteenth century, there were two main Christian traditions in Western Europe:
  - the Catholic Church, led by the Pope
  - the Protestant Church, which consists of many different **denominations**.
- One of the key areas of disagreement between the traditions related to the authority given to the Bible and the authority given to the Church.

> **Exam tip**
>
> You need to understand the different views on the authority of the Church in relation to the authority of the Bible that are found in the Catholic and Protestant traditions. For this, it helps to have an outline knowledge of the history of the western Church from its beginnings in the first century CE to the **Reformation** in the sixteenth century.

Outline of the two different views of the authority of the Bible and the Church

Protestant view	Catholic view
Sola scriptura: the Bible alone has authority	Bible and Tradition are equal in status
Believers interpret what it says to them in their situation through prayer and in the light of their conscience	The Magisterium (the teaching authority of the Church) is the guardian and interpreter of both the Bible and Tradition.

Reformation refers to the split in the Church that occurred in the sixteenth century when individuals and groups protested against what they believed to be wrong teaching and corrupt practice in the Catholic Church.

The **Apostles** (from the Greek word that means 'sent out') were the disciples chosen by Jesus to be with him in his ministry and to continue his work after Jesus' resurrection. A wider group of Christians, including Paul, were also called apostles.

Bishops in the Catholic Church derive their authority from the Apostolic Succession. They are in charge of a group of parishes in a geographical location known as a diocese.

The **Apostolic Succession** refers to the idea that the Apostles passed on their authority to the bishops whom they appointed to succeed them. This passing on of authority from bishops to bishops has continued down the centuries.

The **Pope** is the leader of the Catholic Church and Catholics believe that the Pope's authority can be traced back in a direct line to Peter.

Denomination is a term that refers to a recognised branch of the Christian Church.

Sola scriptura means 'Scripture alone', which is the view of the Protestant denominations.

The Protestant Churches

Martin Luther (1483–1546)

- *Sola scriptura*: the Bible is the only source of religious authority.
- Christians should not say that some parts are true and others are false.
- The Bible gives the standard of measurement for deciding on the truth of Church teachings.
- Without the Bible, there would be no Church.
- This precedence of the Bible over the Church is illustrated in Luther's belief that salvation comes through faith, not through the institutions of the Church and that all Christians have equal access to God through prayer.
- This belief is known as 'the priesthood of all believers' and comes from the New Testament.

The Baptist Church

- Baptists are evangelical Christians, but most are not fundamentalist.
- They combine the *sola scriptura* approach (**special revelation**) with the use by the individual of reason and conscience (**general revelation**).
- The New Testament takes priority over the Old Testament and as the inspired word of God, it provides the standard by which all other teachings should be assessed.
- They reject the authority of the Church as an institution, i.e. of religious tradition, creeds, etc.

The Catholic Church

- The Gospel was passed on in two ways that are equal in status because both were inspired by the Holy Spirit.
- The Bible was passed on in written form by the Apostles and other inspired religious teachers.
- Once the Bible gained its fixed form, it could neither be added to nor taken away from.
- Tradition was passed on in oral form (and eventually written down) by the Apostles. This is known as the Apostolic Tradition.
- It is always in agreement with what is contained in the Bible, though it may contain truths not found in the Bible.
- It is a living form of the truth in that it is added to by new insights, e.g. ethical teachings on bio-medical issues.
- The passing on and interpretation of the Bible and Tradition are overseen by the Magisterium.
- It receives the authority from God to give an interpretation of both the Bible and Tradition that is authentic, and its teachings must be obeyed.

> **Key quotation**
>
> We find the true faith in Sacred Scripture and in the living Tradition of the Church.
>
> Youcat 12

> **Key quotation**
>
> Let us not change the Word of God; we ourselves should be changed through the Word ... It is by the standard of Scripture that the believer is enabled to measure all other teaching.
>
> A Skevington Wood, *Captive to the Word*

> **Key quotation**
>
> You are a chosen race, a royal priesthood.
>
> 1 Peter 2:9

Special revelation refers to the way in which God makes himself known in specific ways/times. The Bible and religious experiences are two forms of special revelation.

General revelation refers to the way in which God makes himself known to people through nature, reason and conscience, for instance. The knowledge of God that may be obtained in this way is available to all people at all times.

Magisterium refers to the teaching authority of the Catholic Church, consisting of the Pope and bishops.

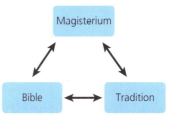

Now test yourself

TESTED ☐

1. What is the Catholic view of the status of the Church in relation to the Bible?
2. What do Catholics mean by the Apostolic Succession?
3. To what does the term Magisterium refer?
4. What do Protestant Christians mean by *sola scriptura*?
5. How did Martin Luther explain the relationship between the Bible and the Church?

The authority of Jesus

Summary of the two different views about the authority of Jesus

Jesus' authority as God's authority:
- based on the claim that Jesus was **God incarnate**.

Jesus' authority as only human:
- based on the claim that Jesus was not divine.

> **Exam tip**
>
> These two ways of understanding the nature of Jesus' authority are not so much denominationally based as based on different understandings of the authority and reliability of the Gospels and on interpretation of the text.

Jesus' authority as God's authority

This is the traditional view as stated in the Nicene Creed and is the official view of almost all Churches. It is based on an acceptance of New Testament claims about Jesus as true.
- According to the Gospels, Jesus claimed to have divine authority.
- That authority was seen in
  - his teaching
  - the miracles attributed to him
  - the titles used by and of Jesus, e.g. Son of God, **Messiah**, Son of Man.

> **Key quotations**
>
> All authority in heaven and on earth has been given to me.
>
> Matthew 28:18
>
> Father, the hour has come. Glorify your Son, that your Son may glorify you. For you granted him authority over all people …
>
> John 17:1–2

God incarnate states the belief that Jesus is God in human form; 'incarnate' means 'in flesh'.

Messiah is a title meaning 'anointed one' that was used for Jewish kings, indicating that they were chosen by God and so were sons of God; Christians believe that Jesus was the Messiah.

Jesus' divine authority seen in his teaching

On one occasion, according to Mark, those who heard Jesus teach were amazed both by what he said and the manner in which he taught. They were used to their religious teachers giving instruction that was based on teachings from previous religious teachers. Jesus, however, taught in a new, direct and original way. He taught with authority, and those who believed in him were convinced that his authority came from God.

> **Key quotation**
>
> The people were amazed at his teaching, because he taught them as one who had authority, not as the teachers of the law.
>
> Mark 1:22

Jesus' divine authority seen in his healing

The emphasis in the story of Jesus healing the centurion's servant is on the amazing faith of the Roman centurion who recognised the absolute authority of Jesus over healing, comparing it to his own authority over the soldiers under him. In the same way that just one word was enough for instant obedience, so Jesus needed only to say the word for healing to take place. But the story also shows that Jesus had a unique authority.

> **Key quotation**
>
> Lord, don't trouble yourself … But say the word, and my servant will be healed. For I myself am a man under authority, with soldiers under me.
>
> Luke 7:6–8

Jesus as Son of God

In the Old Testament, this title was used of kings.
- The phrase 'son of' means 'reflecting the nature of'/'like'.
- Kings were thought to have been adopted by God at their accession.
- They were meant to reflect God's justice and mercy in their rule.
- By the time of Jesus, it was linked with the title of 'Messiah', which also included the idea of being chosen by God to rule on his behalf.

In the New Testament, the title indicates Jesus' unique divine authority.
- At the beginning of Mark's Gospel, Jesus is referred to as the Son of God and he is said to be 'my beloved Son' in the visions at his baptism and transfiguration.

> **Key quotation**
>
> Jesus said, 'All things have been committed to me by my Father. No one knows the Son except the Father, and no one knows the Father except the Son ...
>
> Matthew 11:27

Jesus as Son of Man

In the Old Testament, this was a very ambiguous term.
- It could mean 'I', a human being, a representative of humanity or a supernatural figure bringing God's judgement.

It was Jesus' preferred title for himself.
- Its ambiguity made it less likely that he would be thought of as a power figure and potential revolutionary.
- He used it to describe his role as the 'suffering servant' spoken of in the Old Testament and to his God-given authority both in the present and the future.

> **Key quotations**
>
> I want you to know that the Son of Man has authority on earth to forgive sins.
>
> Mark 2:10
>
> For even the Son of Man did not come to be served, but to serve, and to give his life as a ransom for many.
>
> Mark 10:45
>
> ... you will see the Son of Man sitting at the right hand of the Mighty One ...
>
> Mark 14:62

Jesus' authority as only human

Two groups of Christians take this view:
- Small groups in the early centuries of the Church and in more recent times who interpret texts in a different way from the majority of Christians.
- Liberal Christians who reject any idea of divine inspiration underlying the Bible.

Adoptionism

- The belief that Jesus was not divine by nature.
- God 'adopted' him as his 'son' at the baptism (Mark 1:9–11) in the same way as kings in ancient Israel were thought to be chosen by God as his earthly representatives.

Unitarianism

- This denomination, still in existence, was founded in the eighteenth century.
- It adopts a **deist** view of the creation of the world, i.e. God created the world but then had no further connection with it.
- Jesus was just a spiritual leader so his teachings may contain useful insights, but there is no idea of divine authority attaching to them.

Liberal Christian views

- The Gospels were products of several decades of thinking about the significance of Jesus' life and teaching.
- Jesus' teaching and the stories associated with him had been passed down by word of mouth and would have been altered and even exaggerated in the telling.
- This process can be seen in the Gospels themselves, e.g. in the differing accounts of the calming of the storm that are found in the first three Gospels.
- The influence of Greek philosophy and mystery religions led to the human Jesus being transformed into a divine figure.
- This is reinforced by the outlook of modern science, which rejects the possibility of miracles.
- Jesus, then, was a human being like all other humans, though his deeply spiritual nature gave his teaching authority.

Adoptionism was the belief held by some Christians in the early Church that Jesus was not divine by nature, but was adopted by God at his baptism.

Unitarianism is a small Christian denomination that rejects belief in the divinity of Jesus.

Deist refers to the view that God did not have any further relationship with the world after creating it; deism's belief in God is founded on reason and nature.

Christian responses to the teaching of Jesus

- Those who see Jesus' authority as God's authority will feel they should obey his teaching, but that may not be as simple as it seems; some of his teaching seems to be totally impractical and counter-intuitive.
- Those who regard Jesus' authority as only human are free to decide for themselves whether or not they should follow his teaching.

Christian understandings of Jesus' teaching on retaliation and love for enemies (Matthew 5: 38–48)

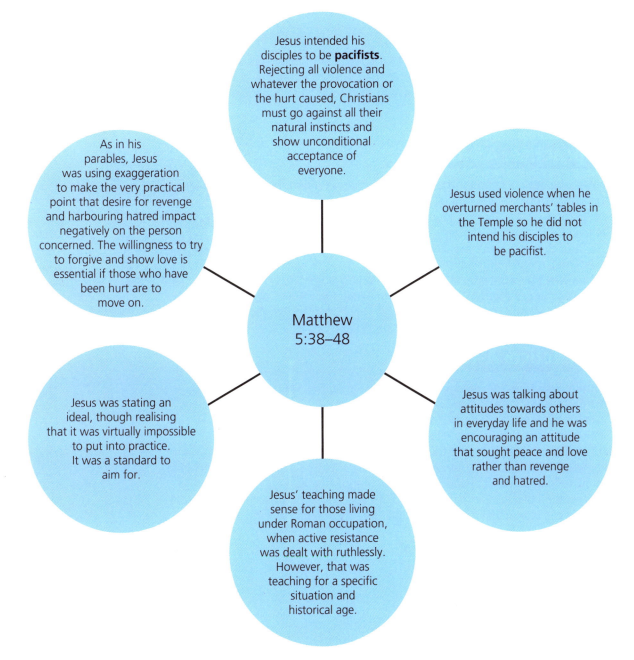

Jesus intended his disciples to be **pacifists**. Rejecting all violence and whatever the provocation or the hurt caused, Christians must go against all their natural instincts and show unconditional acceptance of everyone.

As in his parables, Jesus was using exaggeration to make the very practical point that desire for revenge and harbouring hatred impact negatively on the person concerned. The willingness to try to forgive and show love is essential if those who have been hurt are to move on.

Jesus used violence when he overturned merchants' tables in the Temple so he did not intend his disciples to be pacifist.

Matthew 5:38–48

Jesus was stating an ideal, though realising that it was virtually impossible to put into practice. It was a standard to aim for.

Jesus was talking about attitudes towards others in everyday life and he was encouraging an attitude that sought peace and love rather than revenge and hatred.

Jesus' teaching made sense for those living under Roman occupation, when active resistance was dealt with ruthlessly. However, that was teaching for a specific situation and historical age.

Jesus as a role model

Whatever their view of the nature of Jesus' authority, all Christians see him as a role model.

- They believe that they should seek to emulate his life of self-giving love, which reflected his teaching that the two greatest commandments were love of God and love of neighbour.
- Many non–Christians, such as Gandhi, have been inspired by the teaching and example of Jesus.

> **Pacifists** reject any use of violence; Christian pacifists may base their beliefs on texts such as Matthew 5: 38–42.

Now test yourself

TESTED

1 Which two titles are used in the Gospels to refer to Jesus' divine authority?
2 What do Unitarians believe about the authority of Jesus?
3 Why do some liberal Christians believe that Jesus' authority was only human?
4 Give three ways in which Christians interpret Jesus' teaching to 'turn the other cheek'.
5 What overall attitude do Christians have to the life and teaching of Jesus?

Exam practice: AS-level

1 a Explain the beliefs of one Christian tradition about the authority of the Bible. [15 marks]
  b 'The Bible is inspired by God.' Assess this view. [15 marks]
2 a Explain how Catholic views about the authority of the Church might influence the lives of ordinary Catholics. [15 marks]
  b 'The Church is the most important source of authority for twenty-first century Christians.' Assess this view. [15 marks]
3 a Explain why many Christians believe that Jesus' authority was God's authority. [15 marks]
  b 'Jesus teaching in Matthew 5:33–48 is impossible to follow.' Assess this view. [15 marks]

Exam practice: A-level

1 a Examine two different Christian views concerning the nature of the Bible. [15 marks]
  b 'The Bible is inspired by God.' Evaluate this claim. [15 marks]
2 a Examine different Christian views on the authority of the Church. [10 marks]
  b 'The Church is the most important source of authority for twenty-first century Christians.' Evaluate this claim. [15 marks]
3 a Examine how their belief that Jesus' authority was God's authority influences the attitude of some Christians to his teaching. [10 marks]
  b 'The teaching of Jesus in Matthew 5:33–48 about turning the other cheek makes sense only if Jesus intended it as an ideal.' Evaluate this claim. [15 marks]

2 God

Christian monotheism

One God

- **Monotheism** is the belief held by all Christians that there is only one God.
- In the earliest centuries of Israel's history, the Jews believed that other gods existed, but should not be worshipped. The Sinai covenant makes it clear that Israel's God, the Lord, alone should be worshipped.
- The development of monotheism can be seen in the Old Testament writings of the prophets.

> **Key quotation**
>
> I am the first and I am the last; apart from me there is no God.
>
> Isaiah 44:6

> **Key quotation**
>
> I am the Lord your God, who brought you out of Egypt, out of the land of slavery. You shall have no other gods before me.
>
> Exodus 20:2–3

- The classic statement of monotheism is found in the Jewish statement of faith known as the *Shema*, Deuteronomy 6:4.
- Israel's monotheism was not a philosophical concept, but it applied to life; it was ethical monotheism.
- This was expressed in Israel's obligations as set out in the **Sinai covenant**.

> **Key quotation**
>
> Now if you obey me fully and keep my covenant, then out of all nations you will be my treasured possession.
>
> Exodus 19:5

> **Key quotation**
>
> Hear, O Israel: The Lord our God, the Lord is one.
>
> Deuteronomy 6:4

- These obligations were listed in the Ten Commandments.
- When Jesus was asked which of the commandments was the greatest, he said that love of God and of neighbour were the greatest and summed up the whole of the Jewish religion.

> **Key quotation**
>
> The most important one ... is this: 'Hear, O Israel: The Lord our God, the Lord is one. Love the Lord your God with all your heart and with all your soul and with all your mind and with all your strength.' The second is this: 'Love your neighbour as yourself.' There is no commandment greater than these.
>
> Mark 12:29–31

- **Ethical monotheism**, as seen throughout the New Testament, ties in with Christian beliefs about salvation.

> **Exam tip**
>
> As you revise each of the topics set for study, e.g. God, you should start to see the links with other topics that you have studied in philosophy, ethics and Christianity. Seeing and making such links should enable you to answer exam questions in greater depth. You might like to note them down to refer back to when you are working on the Dialogues.

Monotheism refers to the belief that there is one God.

The **Sinai covenant** refers to the agreement made through Moses between God and Israel; in return for their absolute commitment to God, Israel was to be God's chosen people.

Ethical monotheism means that belief in one God includes also following the moral codes linked to that belief, e.g. the Ten Commandments.

Omnipotent creator and controller of all things

Omnipotence

Most Christians believe that God is **omnipotent**. The idea of omnipotence is understood in different ways.
- Some follow Descartes' view that omnipotence means God can do absolutely anything. This interpretation raises issues relating to the problem of evil.
- Most Christians think that omnipotence means that God is able to do anything that is logically possible. This answers the issue of the problem of evil, but there are further issues relating to free will and determinism.

God as omnipotent Creator

There are three approaches to the belief in God as Creator:
1 A minority of Christians think in terms of the universe as coming out of God's own being. Most, however, reject this identification of God with the created universe because it limits God.
2 The view accepted by many Christians is that the universe was created by God out of nothing (*ex nihilo*). This idea is expressed in the repeated 'Let there be … and there was …' in Genesis 1. His word brought everything into existence and ordered it. It is based on the usual English translation of Genesis 1:1–3.
3 The third approach, using an alternative translation and adopted by process theology, is the view that the earth was already in existence and in a state of chaos. God then worked at ordering it.

God as the omnipotent controller of all things

- The biblical references to God as King express the belief that everything is subject to God's control.
- Most Christians believe that God not only created the universe, he also sustains it.
- The ethical teachings found in the Bible show how God sustains human life in the spiritual as well as the physical sense.
- Most Christians believe that God is **omniscient**. This creates issues both for the problem of evil and for human free will. There are three approaches to the concept of omniscience:
  1 God knows past, present and future absolutely and in a causative sense. This means that he controls everything that goes on in the universe, including human actions. This view is known as **theological determinism**.
  2 Because God exists beyond space and time, **spatio-temporal language** is not appropriate in relation to him, although we have to use it because it is all we have. God simply sees and knows all things, including the free choices that humans make, but his knowledge is not causative. (This was Aquinas' view.)
  3 According to Swinburne, God exists within time and knows all that it is logically possible for God to know. This means he cannot be the cause of human future choices, because he cannot know them, though he might be able to predict them.

Transcendent and unknowable

This refers to the belief of many Christians that God is beyond and outside the world of space and time.
- God is eternal and limitless.
- Catholic teaching refers to God's **aseity**.

The clearest expression of this belief is seen in the call of Moses.
- Moses asked to know God's name, and the reply was 'I am who I am'. In other words, no human can possibly know God's name, i.e. understand what it means to be God.

Omnipotent means all-powerful.

Creation *ex nihilo* refers to the belief that God created the universe out of nothing.

Omniscient means all-knowing.

Theological determinism is the view that God's absolute control of everything means he causes all that happens.

Spatio-temporal language is language related to space and time, e.g. 'fore-knowing'.

Aseity is the belief in God's self-existence; it is his nature to exist.

The doctrine of the Trinity

Many Christians believe that God is 'Three in One'.

- For some Christians, Trinitarian belief is implied in the Old Testament.
- The Hebrew word often used in the Old Testament for God (*Elohim*) is plural.
- In Genesis 1, God as the 'father' of the universe created through his word and his spirit broods over the watery chaos.
- There are clearer hints in the New Testament, e.g. in the baptism of Jesus.

> **Key quotation**
>
> Just as Jesus was coming up out of the water, he saw heaven being torn open and the Spirit descending on him like a dove. And a voice came from heaven: 'You are my Son, whom I love; with you I am well pleased.'
>
> Mark 1:10–11

In the early centuries of the Church's existence, Church leaders considered the implications of:

- biblical texts
- their conviction that Jesus was uniquely the Son of God
- their experience of the power of the Holy Spirit guiding the lives of individual Christians and the life of the Church as a whole.

A number of **heresies** drove them to set out formally the doctrine of the Trinity that is held by most Christian denominations:

- There is one God in three Persons: Father, Son and Holy Spirit.
- Each **Person** possesses fully all the attributes of the Godhead: eternity, omnipotence, omniscience, etc.
- The relationship between the three Persons is one of mutual indwelling.

> **Key quotation**
>
> God is not solitude but perfect communion.
> Pope Benedict XVI, Solemnity of the Most Holy Trinity, May 2005

The importance of the doctrine of the Trinity

For most Christian Churches, belief in the Trinity is important for many reasons, some of which are outlined below.

- The diversity together with unity within creation reflects the diversity within the unity of the Godhead.
- It can be seen as a reflection of the Trinitarian paradox of unity within diversity.
- It connects with Christian beliefs about sin and **atonement**.
- Those Christians who believe in the doctrine of original sin claim that God sent his Son to atone for that sin through his crucifixion and resurrection and so reconcile humans to God; the Holy Spirit works within believers' hearts and lives, giving hope of eternal life.
- The doctrine of the **Trinity** explains the otherwise paradoxical claim that God is both **transcendent** and **immanent**.
- Moltmann described the relationships of the Persons of the Trinity in terms of mutual self-giving and receiving love. This is to be reflected in human relationships.

Heresies are beliefs stated to be false by the leaders of the Christian Church, e.g. adoptionism (see previous chapter).

Person in relation to the Trinity is a translation of the word 'persona' which was used of a mask worn by Greek actors.

Atonement is literally 'at-one-ment'. It refers to the Christian belief that through the death of Christ, the barrier of sin was broken and humans were reconciled to God.

Trinity is literally 'tri-unity' and refers to the Christian belief that God is one nature in three Persons, i.e. is both one and three.

Transcendent refers to the belief that God is without limits and is beyond the world of space and time.

Immanent refers to the belief that God pervades and sustains the universe and that humans are able to have a personal relationship with God.

Jesus as the Son of God

For Christians who believe that Jesus is the second Person of the Trinity, Jesus' authority is God's authority.

> **Exam tip**
>
> Before revising this section on the two set texts, read through again the sections on Jesus as a source of authority in pages 244–248 of your text book and in pages 7–11 of this revision guide.

John 10:30

- This was Jesus' response to those who asked him if he was the Messiah.
- There are two possible ways of understanding the word 'one' in this text.
- 'One' as referring to common essence; 'of one Being with the Father' is the phrase used in the Nicene Creed.
- 'One' as referring to unity of purpose; God's purpose for humanity and Jesus' mission were in harmony.
- Biblical support can be claimed for both these ways.

> **Key quotation**
>
> I and the Father are one.
>
> John 10:30

Unity of essence	Unity of purpose
The idea of pre-existence is present in: John 1:1–2 which states that the Word was in the beginning with God 8:58 where Jesus states 'Before Abraham was, I am'	John 18: where Jesus prays that he and his disciples might be one
The Jews who had asked the question regarded his answer as blasphemous and wanted to stone him to death	In part of his discussion with the Jews, Jesus said that he was simply doing God's work

Further points to consider are:

- Jesus himself spoke Aramaic, so what he said might have been distorted in the translation into Greek.
- John's Gospel was written probably over 60 years after the crucifixion, which gives another possible reason for distortion.
- Many scholars think John's Gospel was an interpretation of the life and teaching of Jesus as recorded in earlier traditions and Gospels.
- One of the reasons for John's Gospel was the need to combat heresy, so this might have 'slanted' the text.

1 Corinthians 8:6

This forms part of Paul's reply to the question raised by Christians in Corinth as to whether it was permissible to eat meat from animals that had been sacrificed in pagan temples. He is here reminding those reading his letter, many of whom were converts from paganism, that monotheism is central to Christian faith. It reads like a statement of belief, so maybe Paul was quoting something in current use in Christian worship. He sets out his teaching on this in a style reminiscent of Hebrew poetry found in the Old Testament, which is structured not on rhyme but on parallelism and rhythm:

Key quotation

... yet for us there is but one God, the Father, from whom all things came and for whom we live; and there is but one Lord, Jesus Christ, through whom all things came and through whom we live.

1 Corinthians 8:6

| One God, the Father | from whom are all things | and for whom we exist |
| One Lord, Jesus Christ | through whom are all things | and through whom we exist |

- Some Christians think that Paul had the *Shema* (as quoted earlier in this chapter) in mind and that he was equating Jesus with God.
- Other Christians think that the use of the preposition 'through' suggests that Jesus was God's agent in creation but not in the sense of being divine.
- There is no way of giving an absolutely definite answer on what is meant by this and other New Testament texts about the status of Jesus.
- It took the Church several centuries of debate to get its thinking clear on this and perhaps such texts represent early steps in that process of thought.

Now test yourself

TESTED ☐

1 What is meant by ethical monotheism?
2 Give two ways of explaining what is meant by omnipotent.
3 What do Christians mean when they refer to God as transcendent?
4 Who are the three Persons of the Trinity?
5 What are the two ways of understanding 'one' in John 10:20?

God as Personal, God as Father and God as Love

The Bible often describes God in **anthropomorphic** terms; for instance, in Genesis 2, God is said to walk in the garden in the cool of the day. At the call of Moses, God tells him that 'I have indeed seen the misery of my people in Egypt … and I am concerned about their suffering' (Exodus 3:7). God is depicted as having human emotions and a human body. This type of language understands God as personal and refers to God in human terms.

God as Personal

REVISED

This refers to the belief that humans can relate to God.
- God is immanent, i.e. involved in the world and accessible.
- God hears and answers prayers.
- This is seen in the indwelling of the Holy Spirit in the spirit of a believer.

> **Key quotation**
>
> … your bodies are temples of the Holy Spirit, who is in you …
>
> 1 Corinthians 6:19

God as Father

REVISED

In the biblical world, this was not just a term relating to the family. The oldest male in the society was responsible for, respected by and had absolute control over the rest of the group. So Old Testament references to God as Father attribute to him a number of roles:
- Creating the universe
- Rescuing Israel when in trouble
- Setting standards of behaviour, e.g. in giving the Ten Commandments
- Exercising justice, rewarding obedience and punishing misdemeanours.

New Testament references include ideas of both protective love and power.

Jesus often referred to God as Father.
- In the parable of the Forgiving Father, God's unconditional and ceaseless love is depicted.
- Jesus tells his disciples that their heavenly Father will give good things to those who ask him and teaches them a prayer that addresses God as 'our Father'.
- Jesus' relationship with God is seen in his prayer in Gethsemane, where he uses Abba, the intimate Aramaic term for Father.

> **Key quotation**
>
> 'Abba, Father,' he said, 'everything is possible for you. Take this cup from me. Yet not what I will, but what you will.'
>
> Mark 14:36

Paul claims that when they pray 'Abba, Father', Christians become adopted children of God.

The **Apostles' Creed** refers to God as Father in two senses: as creator of the universe and as the father of Jesus.

> **Key quotation**
>
> I believe in God, the Father Almighty, maker of heaven and earth; and in Jesus Christ his only Son, our Lord …
>
> Apostles' Creed

> **Anthropomorphic** language refers to language describing God in terms of a human.
>
> The **Apostles' Creed** is, in its current form, a fourth century statement of Christian belief.

God as Love

Philosophically, the reality of evil challenges claims that God is **omnibenevolent**, but Christians nevertheless trust in God's love from their own experience and on the basis of biblical teaching.

> **Omnibenevolent** means all-loving.

- The Old Testament uses the Hebrew term *hesed*, often translated as 'steadfast love', to depict God's dependable commitment to the covenant with Israel.
- The New Testament equivalent of *hesed* is the Greek word *agape*, which denotes God's selfless, self-giving, generous and unconditional love for humanity.
- According to the writer of 1 John, 'God is love' (1 John 4:8).
- *Agape* is part of the nature of the Trinity.

> **Key quotation**
>
> For God so loved the world that he gave his one and only Son, that whoever believes in him shall not perish but have eternal life.
>
> John 3:16

- Because they are created in God's image, human relationships have *agape* at their heart.
  - Hence Jesus' two greatest commandments: love of God and love of neighbour.
  - *Agape* was central to Fletcher's situation ethics, which you studied in Component 1: Philosophy and Ethics. This is discussed in the Dialogues section on page 125.

God as King

Monarchy was a familiar concept for most of the biblical period and whether monarchs ruled small city-states or huge nations, the ruler's authority was absolute. So it is not surprising that 'king' and other royal titles were used of God.

In his vision in the Temple, the prophet Isaiah saw God seated on a throne (the Ark of the Covenant was thought of as God's throne) and he feared he would die, 'for my eyes have seen the King, the Lord of hosts'. The vision is one of God's power over everything, including life and death.

In the previous chapter of this revision guide, there was reference to Jesus as Messiah. The term was used of Israel's kings and so its application to Jesus suggests a kingly figure, associated with power and wealth, which was why Jesus did not use it himself.

Jesus was associated with the inauguration of the Kingdom of God:

- This is not a place but refers to God's rule as King of the universe.
- It is often understood as both a present and a future reality.
- Understood as part of the future reality; Jesus, the anointed King, will return to fully establish the Kingdom of God. In the Kingdom of God there will be no pain or hunger, and there will be peace.

The problems with anthropomorphic language

- Using this kind of language puts limits on a God who is believed to be transcendent.
- The portrayal of God suggests someone like us who is changeable and therefore not reliable; he is therefore not worthy of worship.
- Many Christians, though, would say that the only meaningful way for humans to describe God is to use such language, though they recognise its limitations when applied to a Being who is essentially beyond human understanding. However, this does not solve the issue.
- Many of the metaphors used for God are associated with domination and above all, they are male.

The debate about gender-specific language

- Women feel excluded by the use of gender-specific language that is found throughout the Bible, which is culturally conditioned and reinforces patriarchal stereotypes of male superiority.
- In response to this, some gender-neutral translations of the Bible have been produced. Many hymns and some prayers and forms of worship have been revised.
- However, this does not address the problem highlighted by feminists that the God portrayed in the Bible is a male figure, with all the typically male attributes of power.
  - Such language encourages a distorted and unacceptable understanding of God.
  - The standard gender-neutral translations of the Bible do not apply gender-neutral terms to God.

In an attempt to redress this, many United States divinity faculties are encouraging lecturers to avoid the use of male pronouns when speaking of God and to replace them with words such as 'God' or 'Godself'.

- A post-Christian thinker like Daphne Hampson does likewise, but in her case she also has a rather different conception of 'that which is God'.

In response, other Christians, including some feminist theologians, point to the presence in the Bible and in the thinking of the Church of feminine attributes used of God.

- An early Church theologian (Clement of Alexandria) referred to Christians nursing at the breast of God the Father.
- Meister Eckhart (a medieval mystic) referred to God lying on a maternity bed and giving birth.
- Another medieval mystic, Mother Julian, made frequent references to God in feminine terms, stating that 'as truly as God [the Father] is our Father, so truly is God [the Son] our Mother'.

Other Christians think that to remove all gender-specific references from the Bible would be to lose many insights, as it was a product of its culture and to be properly understood, it needs to be studied in that context.

- The biblical writers deliberately avoided reference to God as Mother because of the prevalence of fertility religions; references to God as Father prevented the infiltration of their beliefs and practices into Jewish and Christian faiths.

There are also feminists who think that attributing 'female' qualities to the male God just compounds the problem. The male now contains all within himself. What is needed is to see women and men, female and male, as equal.

Feminist issues are studied again in a later topic of the specification (Christianity, gender and sexuality).

> **Key quotation**
>
> I have concluded that fundamental to the Abrahamic religions is the will to subvert women and establish man as norm … [in so far as that is the case] these religions are a form of fascism.
>
> Daphne Hampson, Academy Conferences lecture, Oxford, April 2016

> **Key quotation**
>
> For a long time I have kept silent, I have been quiet and held myself back. But now, like a woman in childbirth, I cry out, I gasp and pant.
>
> Isaiah 42:14

Now test yourself

1 What do Christians mean when they say that God is immanent?
2 Why do many Christians refer to God as Father?
3 What is the problem with using anthropomorphic language to describe God?
4 What is the problem for feminists of the biblical depiction of God as king?
5 Why do some Christians think it would be wrong to remove all gender-specific language from the Bible?

The concept of God in process theology

Process theology

REVISED

Process theology, which developed in the twentieth century, originated in the ideas of A.N. Whitehead who was strongly influenced by quantum mechanics' ideas that the sub-atomic world is in a process of continual change. His ideas have been developed further by David Griffin.

God is not the Creator

Griffin rejects the traditional Christian belief in creation out of nothing:
- He adopts the alternative translation of Genesis 1:1–3 that is given earlier in this chapter.
- The universe has always existed; it is uncreated and eternal.
- It was therefore not created by God.
- God, like the universe, is uncreated and eternal.
- The relationship between God and the universe is **panentheistic**.
  - They exist together just as the human mind and human body exist together.
  - The universe is in God and God is in the universe.
- God's role in relation to the universe is to persuade it into order and complexity.
  - This attempt has gone on for 13.7 billion years, using the processes of the Big Bang and of evolution.
  - The world's independence of God explains the very slow and arduous progress.

> **Panentheistic** is the adjective used by process theology to describe the relationship between God and the universe. God and the universe exist together in the way that human minds and bodies exist together. Everything is in God and God is immanent in the universe.

God is not omnipotent

- God does not have unlimited power. This follows on from his views on God's relation to the world.
- Because it is independent of God, the ever-changing chaotic matter making up the universe is able to resist God's attempts at persuasion.

Assessment of process theology

REVISED

Positives of process theology

- It has support from quantum mechanics.
- It fits in with the theories of Big Bang and evolution.
- It is supported by one possible translation of the Hebrew in Genesis 1.
- It gives an explanation for why God does not control evil: he cannot.
- It claims probability rather than certainty for its views, so it is not a 'closed book'.

Negatives of process theology

The solution to the problem of evil is for many people its most attractive feature, but it comes at a huge cost.
- Its claim that God is not omnipotent goes against what many people, not just Christians, imagine a divine being should be.
- A God who is not omnipotent would be not truly God and not a God worthy of worship in the eyes of many Christians.

Now test yourself

TESTED

1 In what two ways are God and the universe similar?
2 What word describes the relationship between God and the world?
3 What does that word mean?
4 What is God's role in relation to the universe?
5 What does process theology believe about the power of God?

Exam practice: AS-level

1	a Explain Christian beliefs about God as the omnipotent creator of all things.	[15 marks]
	b 'From a Christian point of view, God is unknowable.' Assess this view.	[15 marks]
2	a Explain different Christian views on depicting God as personal.	[15 marks]
	b 'The use of anthropomorphic language helps Christians to understand the nature of God.' Assess this view.	[15 marks]
3	a Explain the views of process theology about God's relationship with the universe.	[15 marks]
	b The concept of God in process theology is not Christian.' Assess this view.	[15 marks]

Exam practice: A-level

1	a Examine the importance for many Christians of belief in the Trinity.	[10 marks]
	b 'Belief in monotheism is incompatible with belief in the Trinity'. Evaluate this claim.	[15 marks]
2	a Examine different Christian views on depicting God as personal.	[10 marks]
	b 'The use of anthropomorphic language helps Christians to understand the nature of God.' Evaluate this claim.	[15 marks]
3	a Examine the differences between traditional Christian views and those of process theology about God's relationship to the world.	[10 marks]
	b 'The concept of God in process theology is not Christian.' Evaluate this claim.	[15 marks]

3 Self, death and afterlife

The meaning and purpose of life

At some point(s) in their lives, most people wonder about the meaning of life in general and, in particular, about what purpose their individual lives have. They draw on their personal experiences and they may be influenced by the views of those they respect and admire. Christians also tend to look for answers or guidance in the beliefs and teachings of their religion, referring to the sources of authority that were considered in the first chapter of this revision guide and in the text book.

To glorify God and have a personal relationship with him

Christians believe that humans cannot know the nature of God. (Refer back to the consideration of God as transcendent and unknowable in the text book and in the previous chapter of this revision guide.)

- The Old Testament writings often refer to God's glory.
- God's **glory** was, according to John's Gospel, reflected uniquely in Jesus.
- Christians believe that because they, like all humans, are created in the image of God (Genesis 1:27), they should reflect God's glory in their lives.
- Jesus taught his disciples that their lives should encourage others to give glory to God.

> **Key quotation**
>
> In the same way, let your light shine before others, that they may see your good deeds and glorify your Father in heaven.
>
> Matthew 5:16

- Living a life that glorifies God means that Christians experience the **Kingdom of God** in this life as well as beyond death.

> **Key quotation**
>
> Very truly I tell you, whoever hears my word and believes him who sent me has eternal life and will not be judged but has crossed over from death to life.
>
> John 5:24

To prepare for judgement

- According to the creation story in Genesis 2, humans were created for fellowship with God, but disobeying God led to alienation.
- God alone could restore the relationship and he did this through the death of Jesus, the supreme act of reconciliation.
- The final act of this reconciliation is the **judgement** that all humans will face.

- Jesus taught in his parable of the sheep and the goats (Matthew 25:31–46) that this would be based on how people responded or failed to respond to those in need.
- Heaven can therefore be seen as a reward for good behaviour, which links to the idea of justification by works.

Glory refers to the infinite beauty and splendour of God.

The **Kingdom of God** is not a geographical location. It refers to the rule of God.

Judgement refers to the traditional Christian belief that after death, people's lives will be assessed by God.

To bring about God's Kingdom on earth

The concept of the Kingdom of God was a key part of Jewish thinking, and in the time of Jesus, there were several ways of thinking about it:

- Jewish rabbis (teachers) thought of the Kingdom as linked to the keeping of the Torah (all 613 commandments set out in the Law). The Kingdom would, however, be brought about by God.
- Many Jews of Jesus' day thought of it in terms of the coming of the Messiah as a military figure who would liberate Israel from Roman occupation.
- Christians believe that Jesus inaugurated the Kingdom.
- Some Christians think of it as an event entirely in the future, linking it to their belief in the Second Coming of Jesus and Judgement Day, referring to Jesus' teaching in the parable of the sheep and the goats.
- Other Christians believe that although the Kingdom will be fully realised after death, it is also a partial reality now.

> **Key quotation**
>
> 'The time has come,' he said. 'The kingdom of God has come near. Repent and believe the good news!'
>
> Mark 1:15

> **Key quotation**
>
> When we pray, 'Thy kingdom come', we call for Christ to come again, as he promised, and for God's reign, which has already begun here on earth, to prevail definitively.
>
> Youcat 520

YouCat is the Youth Catechism of the Catholic Church.

- Yet others see it as their purpose to live in such a way that the values of the Kingdom are realised fully on earth:
  1. This links to the concept of stewardship, which Christians understand as the responsibility of caring not only for their fellow humans but for the whole of God's creation.
  2. The Old Testament prophets spoke of a new age marked by justice, peace and the fulfilment of everyone's needs.
  3. The eighth century prophet Hosea envisaged God making a new covenant with the whole of creation.
  4. Instead of waiting for God to intervene, humans are called to work actively for the realisation of the Kingdom on earth by pursuing justice, etc.

> **Key quotation**
>
> [Christians] are sent to engage in society so that the kingdom of God can grow among men.
>
> Youcat 139

This understanding of the purpose of life does not exclude the more personal approaches seen above.

- Many of those most actively involved in working for the realisation of God's Kingdom on earth see it as a means of giving glory to God.
- What they do arises out of their personal relationship with God, sustained by prayer and meditation.

Now test yourself

1. Outline two Christian views on the nature and purpose of life.
2. In whom, according to John's Gospel, was God's glory uniquely revealed?
3. What, according to Genesis 2, led humans to become alienated from God?
4. To what does the Kingdom of God refer?
5. What do Christians mean when they say 'Thy kingdom come'?

Resurrection

Concept of the soul

In the early Church, Christians tended to combine Jewish ideas with those of Neo-Platonism; the latter were widely accepted in the first-century Mediterranean world.

Jewish thinking

> **Key quotation**
>
> Then the Lord God formed a man from the dust of the ground and breathed into his nostrils the breath of life, and the man became a living being.
>
> Genesis 2:7

- In the Old Testament there are two Hebrew words for soul, *nephesh* and *ruach*.
- They are associated with the principle of life.
- The *nephesh* was said to be given by God to Adam.
- The word is often linked with the word 'heart', which was thought of as the seat of the will.
- In the teaching of Jesus also, the word is often used alongside 'heart' and 'mind', almost in the sense of 'inner self'.

Greek thinking

Plato thought there were two spheres of reality:

- The imperfect world, in which humans live and have only a partial understanding of reality and truth.
- The world of **Forms**.
- The body perishes at death but the soul is immortal and after death is returned to the world of Forms before experiencing **reincarnation**.

Modern thinking

- Many Christians think of the soul as the moral and spiritual dimension of human life – distinct from the physical body. The soul is given by God before birth, and after death it returns to God. This is known as **dualism**.
- Others think of humans in a holistic sense, the physical and mental/spiritual dimensions being inextricably linked and both perishing at death.
- Psychologists use the term 'psyche' to refer to what makes a person an individual.

> **Forms** refers to Plato's theory that everything in the physical universe is a particular and imperfect instance of a perfect idea in the metaphysical world of Forms.
>
> **Reincarnation** is the belief that at death, the soul is separated from the body and is 're-enfleshed' into another body.
>
> **Dualistic** in relation to the concept of the soul means that the soul is thought of as a totally separate entity from the body, from which it separates at death.

The resurrection of Jesus

Belief in life after death was a late development in Jewish thinking in the Old Testament era, and was not a prominent belief in Judaism, but belief in the resurrection of Jesus was from the very start and still is, for most Christians, a central tenet of the Christian faith for a number of reasons:

- It forms the basis of the Christian hope of life after death.
- Paul expressed memorably the sheer pointlessness of life and faith if the resurrection of Jesus is a fiction (see key quotation below).
- All four gospels state that the tomb was empty:
  - All accounts of the resurrection appearances have in common the fact that his friends knew it was Jesus, though not necessarily immediately.
  - He was the same, yet different, and not subject to human limitations.
- It was a unique event.
  - Those whom Jesus was said to have raised to life would in the future have faced death again.
  - Jesus through God's power conquered death, which opened up the possibility of eternal life after death for humanity.
- Christians interpret this idea of resurrection for humanity in different ways:
  - Some think in terms of physical resurrection.
  - Others think in terms of spiritual resurrection.

> **Key quotation**
>
> And if Christ has not been raised, your faith is futile … If only for this life we have hope in Christ, we are of all people most to be pitied.
>
> 1 Corinthians 15:17–19

Resurrection of the flesh according to the writings of Augustine (354–430 CE)

REVISED ☐

Augustine believed that the Fall (described in Genesis 3) affected not only Adam and Eve but also the whole of humanity.

- Every human is infected with sin in every aspect of his/her being: physical, mental, emotional and spiritual.
- Humans are totally dependent on God's grace to deliver them from the eternal punishment that sin merits.
- Christ's saving death achieved atonement and his physical resurrection showed to believers what was a possibility for those whom God had chosen.
- Jesus' resurrection and ascension were physical.
- Augustine believed that God could perform the same miracle for anything created with a soul.
- In this physical resurrection, both the spiritual and physical effects of sin would be erased.
- Augustine's thinking can be seen in the Catholic Church's teaching about resurrection.

Key quotation

… the world has come to believe that the earthly body of Christ was received up into heaven. Already both the learned and unlearned have believed in the resurrection of the flesh and its ascension to the heavenly places …

St Augustine, *City of God*

Key quotation

God created us with a body (flesh) and a soul. At the end of the world he does not drop the 'flesh' like an old toy. On the 'Last Day', he will remake all creation […] this means that we will be transformed but still experience ourselves in *our element*. For Jesus, too, being in the flesh was not just a phase. When the risen Lord showed himself, the disciples saw the wounds on his body.

Youcat 153

Adult butterfly

Eggs

Chrysalis / Cocoon

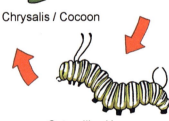

Caterpillar / Larvae

Spiritual resurrection

REVISED ☐

Some Christians reject the idea of a physical resurrection.

- They believe that after death, the body decomposes in a grave or is destroyed by cremation.
- They believe that the soul survives death and lives on with God.
- They believe in a 'spiritual resurrection', along the lines of what Paul taught.
- To explain the idea they might use the analogy of the life cycle of the butterfly.
- The various stages of the life cycle are physically totally different, yet the essential identity is the same.

The significance of 1 Corinthians 15:42–44, 50–54

Key quotation

So will it be with the resurrection of the dead. The body that is sown is perishable, it is raised imperishable; it is sown in dishonour, it is raised in glory; it is sown in weakness, it is raised in power; it is sown a natural body, it is raised a spiritual body. If there is a natural body, there is also a spiritual body. ...

I declare to you, brothers and sisters, that flesh and blood cannot inherit the kingdom of God, nor does the perishable inherit the imperishable. Listen, I tell you a mystery: We will not all sleep, but we will all be changed – in a flash, in the twinkling of an eye, at the last trumpet. For the trumpet will sound, the dead will be raised imperishable, and we will be changed. For the perishable must clothe itself with the imperishable, and the mortal with immortality. When the perishable has been clothed with the imperishable, and the mortal with immortality, then the saying that is written will come true: 'Death has been swallowed up in victory.'

1 Corinthians 15:42–44, 50–54

On the basis of his belief in Jesus' resurrection as set out earlier in 1 Corinthians 15, Paul believed that Jesus' death and resurrection had freed humans from the power of sin and death and had opened up for humanity the possibility of eternal life in the presence of God.

- He believed in resurrection of the body rather than immortality of the soul:
  - not the resurrection of the physical earthly body; that body perished at death
  - rather, a new spiritual and imperishable body, appropriate to the new mode of existence after death.
- He believed that the Second Coming of Christ and the end of the world of human experience were imminent:
  - He describes this in language that many Christians believe was meant as metaphor, showing the momentous nature of what would happen.
  - The trumpet heralds the arrival of a king.

Now test yourself

TESTED

1. Explain the dualist concept of the soul.
2. Give two reasons why belief in resurrection is very important for most Christians.
3. Why do some Christians reject belief in a physical resurrection?
4. Why do some Christians think that the life cycle of the butterfly reflects the resurrection?
5. What did Paul teach about the nature of the resurrection body?

Different interpretations of judgement, heaven, hell and purgatory

Christian teaching

REVISED

The Nicene Creed sets out the belief in judgement and the afterlife.

> **Key quotation**
>
> He will come again in glory to judge the living and the dead, and his kingdom will have no end [...] We look for the resurrection of the dead, and the life of the world to come.
>
> Nicene Creed

The Catholic Church believes that:

- there are two types of judgement after death: **particular judgement** and **general judgement**
- particular judgement refers to the judgement that takes place straight after death and determines the eternal fate of the individual
- the general judgement will take place at the Second Coming of Christ and is upon humanity as a whole
- those who are free from sin are directed immediately to the eternal joys of God's presence in heaven
- those who knowingly and deliberately reject God's love and mercy and those who have committed **mortal sin** and have not repented of it and sought God's forgiveness are directed to hell, which is the state of eternal separation from God
- those whose **venial sins** have not been remitted are directed to **purgatory**, where they will be prepared for heaven

There are three ways of looking at judgement, heaven, hell and purgatory: as physical, as spiritual, and as psychological realities.

Particular judgement refers to the idea held by some that judgement occurs immediately after death.

General judgement refers to the final judgement believed by some to occur at the end of time.

Mortal sins are very serious sins, e.g. murder, that will result in eternal separation from God if those who commit them do not seek God's forgiveness.

Venial sins are less serious sins that do not lead to eternal separation from God.

Purgatory is the mainly Catholic idea of an intermediate state after death in which those destined for heaven are purified of venial sin to make them fit for heaven.

Judgement, heaven, hell and purgatory as physical

REVISED

This was the view almost universally held in the West until modern times. The powerful, both in the Church and in the secular world, saw it as a way of controlling the peasants. Some fundamentalist Christians still believe in it, though any Protestants who think this way reject the idea of purgatory.

- At the end of the world, Christ will return in glory to judge all humans according to their deeds.
- Those assessed as holy will be taken to heaven (often depicted as a city) by angels.
- Those who have committed mortal sins will be cast into hell to suffer torment, often depicted as blazing fire, for eternity.
- Those whose sins are venial undergo a period of cleansing suffering and pain (known as purgatory) and this will enable them to enter heaven.

> **Key quotation**
>
> Then I saw a great white throne and [Christ] who was seated on it. The earth and the heavens fled from his presence, and there was no place for them. [...] The dead were judged according to what they had done as recorded in the books.
>
> Revelation 20:11–12

Judgement, heaven, hell and purgatory as spiritual

REVISED

For those who believe in resurrection as spiritual rather than physical, ideas of judgement, heaven, hell and purgatory as physical realities do not make sense. Many Christians therefore understand them as spiritual realities.

Modern Catholic thinking, for instance, understands heaven, hell and purgatory as spiritual rather than physical realities. The view of judgement is similar to that of the Eastern Churches, with a two-fold judgement.

- Heaven is a spiritual state.
- Likewise, hell is not a physical realm of torture. It results from the deliberate choice of mortal sin without repentance and refusing God's offer of forgiveness.
- Purgatory is not a place.

> **Key quotation**
>
> The so-called particular or personal judgement occurs at the moment of death of the individual. The general judgement, which is also called the Last Judgement, occurs on the Last Day, at the end of the world, when the Lord comes again.
>
> Youcat 157

> **Key quotations**
>
> Heaven is the endless moment of love. Nothing more separates us from God …
>
> Youcat 158
>
> Hell is the condition of everlasting separation from God, the absolute absence of love.
>
> Youcat 161
>
> Purgatory … is actually a condition. Someone who … still needs purification before he can see God face to face is in purgatory.
>
> Youcat 159

Other Christians reject the idea of particular and general judgement, because that is the language of space and time, which ends at death. There can be only one spiritual judgement, which takes place at death. For the same reason, they reject belief in purgatory.

Judgement, heaven, hell and purgatory as psychological realities

REVISED

Some Christians reject any belief in life after death as it lacks empirical evidence. They think in terms of living in such a way as to bring heaven on earth. Others think of judgement, heaven and hell as products of the human mind. Whichever view is held, joy and unhappiness ('heaven' and 'hell') may be experienced as psychological realities.

- A life lived in accordance with one's convictions is spiritually fulfilled and so the individual experiences joy, etc.
- The opposite is true for one whose life is one of inner conflict and this may lead to the need for psychotherapy.

Objective immortality in process thought

In process theology:

1 God and the universe are uncreated and eternal.
   ○ God did not create the universe out of nothing; his purpose has always been to create order and complexity from chaotic and formless matter.
2 God is not omnipotent.
   ○ He seeks to achieve his purpose through 'persuasion', leading to intelligent, complex beings.
3 God and the universe exist panentheistically.
   ○ God is the soul of the universe, so God experiences every single process within the universe.

These beliefs affect ideas about life after death.

● Most process theologians believe in **objective immortality**. That is, after death, all individual beings (human and animal) remain eternally as 'objects' in the mind of God. In that sense, they never die.
● Process theologians reject the idea of **subjective immortality**, which is the belief held by most Christians that after death, humans exist as thinking subjects with continued experiences, etc.

Process theology avoids the anthropocentrism of much Christian thought about this life and life after death but many people, Christian and non-Christian, reject the idea of objective immortality because:

● it is meaningless. If a person no longer has individual experiences, what significance can being in the mind of God have for that person?
● one feature of life after death for Christians is that innocent suffering will be redeemed. If a person no longer exists as an individual but simply as an object in the mind of God, there will be no awareness of this having been done.

> **Objective immortality** refers to the belief of process theology that after death, all living things exist for ever in the mind of God.
>
> **Subjective immortality** refers to the belief of most Christians that the thinking self continues as the same subject of consciousness.

Now test yourself

1 What does it mean for God to be the soul of the universe?
2 What do process theologians mean by objective immortality?
3 What is meant by subjective immortality?
4 What flaw in much Christian thinking does process theology's view on life after death avoid?
5 Why do many Christians think the idea of objective immortality is meaningless?

Exam practice: AS-level

1 a Explain Christian views on the meaning and purpose of life. [15 marks]
  b 'The most important purpose of life for Christians is to prepare for judgement.' Assess this view. [15 marks]
2 a Explain the significance of Paul's teaching in 1 Corinthians on resurrection. [15 marks]
  b 'The resurrection Christians look forward to is not one of the flesh, it is only spiritual.' Assess this view. [15 marks]
3 a Explain the influence of Christian beliefs about judgement in different Christian traditions. [15 marks]
  b 'Traditional beliefs about resurrection give more hope to people than objective immortality in process thought.' Assess this view. [15 marks]

Exam practice: A-level

1 a Examine Christian views on the meaning and purpose of life. [10 marks]
  b 'The most important purpose of life for Christians is to prepare for judgement.' Evaluate this claim. [15 marks]
2 a Examine why there are different views in Christianity on the nature of the resurrection. [10 marks]
  b 'The resurrection Christians look forward to is not one of the flesh, it is only spiritual.' Evaluate this claim. [15 marks]
3 a Examine different Christian understandings of heaven, hell and purgatory. [10 marks]
  b 'Traditional beliefs about resurrection give more hope to people than objective immortality in process thought.' Evaluate this claim. [15 marks]

4 Good conduct and key moral principles

Good conduct

The importance of good moral conduct in the Christian way of life

REVISED

Christians agree that good conduct is important, though, as seen in the ethics component, they do not agree on how to go about putting it into practice. There are also a range of differing views about why good conduct matters:

- Christians should obey the teachings contained in the Bible which is the word of God.
- The Kingdom of God will be realised on earth through the way in which Christians care for others.
- Christians give glory to God by the way in which they live.
- Individual good conduct will be rewarded with eternal life in heaven.

In the sixteenth century, western Christianity was torn apart by the Reformation. There were bitter disputes that resulted in all-out war between the Catholic Church and the Protestant Churches that came into being.

One area of disagreement was concerned with **justification**; what Christians need to do to be accepted by God and welcomed into his Kingdom.

Three particular ideas, each of which claims support from New Testament teaching, are set for study:

- Justification by faith
- Justification by works
- **Predestination**.

> **Key quotation**
>
> We are here on earth in order to know and to love God, to do good according to his will, and to go someday to heaven.
>
> Youcat 1

> **Justification** means being counted as righteous before God.
>
> **Predestination** is the belief that all events, including the fate of humans after death, have been decided by God from eternity.
>
> **Eschatological** is a term referring to events at the end of time.

Justification by faith

REVISED

The word 'justify' is the translation of a Greek word that had legal connotations.

- In the thinking of Paul and of the sixteenth century reformer, Martin Luther, 'to be justified' means to be counted by God as righteous and so able to have a relationship with God.
- It is an **eschatological** term, which means it is concerned with the ultimate fate of humanity,

Justification by faith in the thinking of Paul

The most important teaching on this concept is found in Paul's letter to the Church in Rome.

- Before his conversion, Paul believed that he had to earn a good relationship with God through keeping the Jewish Law. He was continually frustrated by his inability to do this; the more he tried, the more he seemed to fail.

> **Key quotation**
>
> I have the desire to do what is good, but I cannot carry it out. For I do not do the good I want to do, but the evil I do not want to do – this I keep on doing.
>
> Romans 7:18–19

- Because of **original sin**, it is impossible for humans to earn a good relationship with God.
- Only God's grace makes this possible.
- Humans are invited to respond to God's offer of salvation and eternal life with faith.
- It is not that faith justifies a believer: God alone can justify. The faith of the believer is simply the response to the gift of **grace**.
- The believer is then at peace with God and is able to live a life pleasing to God, but this arises out of the new relationship with God; it is not a way of earning that relationship.
- This has always been the case, even for those who lived before Jesus – such as Abraham.

Original sin refers to the flawed and sinful nature possessed by all humanity. Augustine and Calvin believed that unless aided by God, humans are incapable of doing anything that is good.

Grace refers to the generous and freely given love of God. Augustine and Calvin linked this to the Atonement, whereas Pelagius linked it to God's gift of free will.

Sola fide is a Latin term meaning 'by faith alone'. It refers to the belief of Martin Luther and of many Protestants that justification is by faith alone and not by works.

> **Key quotation**
>
> Abram believed the Lord, and he credited it to him as righteousness.
>
> Genesis 15:6

Justification by faith in the thinking of Martin Luther

Martin Luther set the Reformation in motion in 1517, attacking the corruption in much of the medieval Catholic Church.

- He set out a simpler religion that was based on scripture and the personal faith of the individual believer.
- He proclaimed the doctrine of *sola fide*.
- He taught that the faith of the believer is passive; justification comes by what God achieves through the atoning death of Jesus.
- For Luther, good conduct was the expression of a person's faith, but it had no saving value whatsoever.

> **Key quotation**
>
> Thus a Christian, being consecrated by his faith, does good works; but he is not by these works made ... more of a Christian. That is the effect of faith alone.
>
> Martin Luther, *Concerning Christian Liberty*

> **Typical mistake**
>
> Students often confuse the sixteenth century reformer Martin Luther with the twentieth century American civil rights leader Martin Luther King. Make sure that you avoid that mistake as examiners will not be impressed.

Justification by works

REVISED

The biblical basis for this belief is the New Testament letter of James. The author pointed out that:
- faith on its own is useless
  - It doesn't keep a poor person warm.
  - Even demons believe in God.
- faith is expressed through works
  - This was seen in Abraham's willingness to sacrifice his son for God.
  - It was also seen in the protection of Joshua's spies by a prostitute in order to assist the Israelite conquest of Jericho.

Many Christians accept the need for works because of Jesus' teaching in the parable of the sheep and the goats.
- Judgement will be based on the individual human's help for or failure to help those in need.
- No mention is made of faith; indeed the judgement being carried out is universal; 'before him will be gathered all nations'.

In the Sermon on the Mount, Jesus also stressed the importance of doing God's will.

> **Key quotation**
>
> As the body without the spirit is dead, so faith without deeds is dead.
>
> James 2:26

> **Key quotation**
>
> Not everyone who says to me, 'Lord, Lord,' will enter the kingdom of heaven, but only the one who does the will of my Father who is in heaven.
>
> Matthew 7:21

Justification by faith and works

REVISED

This was the position taken by the Catholic Church at the Counter-Reformation, which was its response to the Protestant Reformation. It stated that some human effort had to be put into the process of justification:
- Justification is God's gift to humanity.
- It is given through the atoning death of Jesus and through baptism (see Chapter 5 for the significance of baptism).
- The power of the Holy Spirit enables us to live good lives.
- Responding to God's grace by living in a way that pleases God is an integral part of the process of salvation.

> **Key quotations**
>
> This righteousness is given through faith in Jesus Christ to all who believe …
>
> Romans 3:22
>
> Through the Holy Spirit … we die to sin and are born to new life in God. The divine gifts of faith, hope, and charity come over us and make us able to live in the light and to obey God's will.
>
> Youcat 337

Predestination

This doctrine, that God has decided who will be justified (and saved) and who will not, is based on the belief that God is omnipotent and omniscient.

Predestination in the teaching of Paul

Paul's letter to the Romans seems to imply that God has decided in advance who would be justified. But many Christians think that this is a distortion of Paul's teaching.

- For Paul, God's purposes could not be known or understood by humans.
- Paul may have simply been trying to say that because he is omniscient, God knows what individuals will freely choose and so in that sense salvation is predestined.

Predestination in the teaching of Augustine

Augustine believed that God infallibly knows who will be saved:

- Predestination is an act of grace; human goodness is the result and not the cause of **election**.
- Humans cannot understand the will of God, i.e. why he chooses to save some and not others.
- God predestines some to his Kingdom whilst leaving others in their sinful state to be consigned to hell as a punishment for their sinful choices and actions.
- Pelagius opposed Augustine, claiming that belief in predestination was incompatible with belief in free will but the Church sided with Augustine.

> **Election** in relation to Calvin's teaching refers to God's choice of some for salvation.
>
> **Double predestination** refers to the Calvinist belief that God both chose some humans for salvation and condemned others to eternal damnation.

Predestination in the teaching of Calvin

- Calvin took Augustine's thinking to its logical conclusion in his teaching about **double predestination**.
- God decided before creation who would be saved and who would be damned to hell.
- Because of original sin, all humanity deserves damnation, so God's act of electing some is entirely an act of grace.

Key quotation

All are not created on equal terms, but some are preordained to eternal life, others to eternal damnation.

Calvin, *The Institutes of the Christian Religion*, Book III, Ch. XXI, Sec. 5

Assessment of the doctrine of predestination

The Catholic Church rejects Calvin's teaching.

> **Key quotation**
>
> God predestines no one to go to hell; for this, a wilful turning away from God (a mortal sin) is necessary, and persistence in it until the end.
>
> Catechism of the Catholic Church 1037

Many Christians oppose the doctrine of predestination on different grounds:

1 The doctrine makes God unjust.

Calvin's response was that humans cannot presume to understand God's will, and in any case the evil actions of the damned show that God's decision was just.

2 It cannot be reconciled with Jesus' portrayal of God as unconditionally merciful, forgiving and loving.

The Calvinist response would be that no one merits salvation, so God's saving anyone at all is a display of his mercy, forgiveness and love.

3 It cannot be reconciled with the concept of free will, as if God foreknows our actions, then we have no choice to obey or disobey his will.

One response to this is to point out that God's omniscience is not causative.

Now test yourself

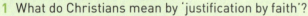

TESTED ☐

1 What do Christians mean by 'justification by faith'?
2 What do Christians mean by 'justification by works'?
3 Why do many Christians believe in 'justification by faith and works'?
4 Give a brief summary of Calvin's teaching on predestination.
5 Give three reasons why many people reject the doctrine of predestination.

Sanctity of life

The concept of the sanctity of life

REVISED

The concept of the sanctity of life is central to Christian thinking about many ethical issues.

For most Christians, this refers only to human life, and gives it **intrinsic value**. This means that the life of a severely disabled newborn baby or a severely demented old person has the same value for God and should be shown the same respect by other people as that of a Nobel prizewinner or a world record-breaking athlete.

It is based on Genesis 1:26–27 and 2:7.
- The first of these states that humans are created in the image of God.
- The second states that when God breathed the breath (*nephesh*) of life into him, the man became a living being (*nephesh chayya*); *nephesh* is often translated as 'soul'.

In Christianity, the **Sanctity of Life** principle takes two forms: the strong principle and the weak.
- According to the strong Sanctity of Life principle, all humans have an absolute right to life that must never be taken away, e.g. by abortion or euthanasia.
- According to the weak form of the principle, all human life is indeed sacred, but it is not absolutely so.
  - In exceptional circumstances, potentially life-saving or preserving treatment may be omitted or withdrawn.
  - The weak form of the principle is often combined with the **Quality of Life** principle, which takes into account a person's capacity for self-fulfilment and dignity of life, etc.

> **Intrinsic value** means that something has value for its own sake.
>
> **Sanctity of life** refers to the belief that life is holy and infinitely precious.
>
> **Quality of life** refers to the capacity for self-fulfilment and the possession of dignity in life.

Applying the Sanctity of Life principle

REVISED

The specification requires that you study this in relation to issues relating to the embryo and the unborn child (i.e. to embryo research and abortion).

> **Exam tip**
>
> You might find it helpful at this point to read again about embryo research and abortion in the Ethics sections of the text book and the Philosophy and Ethics revision guide. However, do remember that the focus of application here is different.

> **Typical mistake**
>
> Many students confuse the terms 'conception' and 'contraception' and state that 'life begins at contraception'. Make sure that you write the correct term.

Strong Sanctity of Life principle

This view is held by Catholics and some Protestants.

In this view, personhood begins at conception.
- This is because at the point of fertilisation, a new life comes into existence with a complete genetic blueprint.
- There is a continuous development of each life from conception to birth.
- From conception, there is an absolute right to life and protection.

This view is supported by scripture, such as when God told Jeremiah that he knew him before he was born.

Although the intentions of embryo research are good, they cannot justify an act that in itself is wrong; the end can never justify the means. Embryo research is considered sinful for the following reasons:

- It exploits the inability of the embryo to give consent.
- It disobeys the biblical teaching to protect the most vulnerable in society.
- The destruction of embryos is tantamount to murder.
- The use of **PGD** is an act of discrimination and could lead to designer babies.

Direct abortion is a grave offence because it is the unlawful (in the eyes of the Church) killing of a person.

Weak Sanctity of Life principle

This view is held by the Church of England and many Protestants.

In this view, from fertilisation, the newly conceived being has the right to respect because of its potential to become a living human being.

- It is a potential person rather than an actual one.
- Its right to life becomes stronger as it develops.

Providing strict controls, such as the 14 days cut-off point, are in place, the Church of England teaches that embryo research is morally acceptable.

- It is an extension of Jesus' healing ministry and a responsible use of God-given skills.
- PGD is acceptable providing it is used for medical reasons only, i.e. preventing the transmission of serious genetic diseases.

The Church of England views abortion as a great moral evil, but states that sometimes it might be the lesser of two evils.

- When the woman's life is at risk or there would be serious permanent harm to her health.
- When the pregnancy has resulted from rape.
- When the resulting child would probably suffer from a terrible life-limiting condition.

PGD is an acronym for pre-implantation genetic diagnosis; it refers to a technique used to test IVF embryos for genetic diseases.

Direct abortion refers to the deliberate termination of a pregnancy, where the death of the embryo/foetus is the intended result.

Assessment of the Sanctity of Life principle

Positives of the Sanctity of Life principle

- It promotes respect for human life.
- It encourages protection of the vulnerable.
- It is true to the teaching of Jesus on *agape* and compassion.
- The weak form recognises that moral decision-making is a complex issue and that opting for abortion may be an act of desperation.

Negatives of the Sanctity of Life principle

- It ignores modern science which states that humans are simply evolved animals.
- It promotes an anthropocentric view of the universe, which devalues animals, etc.
- Its views on abortion, even in the weak form, promote the patriarchal view of society in which women do not have equal rights to men.
- In its strong form, it can seem unloving and lacking in compassion.

The Just War theory

REVISED

Belief in the sanctity of life underlies the Christian version of the Just War theory.

- In its very early history, the Church was largely pacifist.
- Over the centuries, the Just War theory was developed, largely by Augustine and Aquinas.
- There are two main parts to the theory:
  - *Ius ad bellum*, which addresses the conditions when going to war might be justifiable
  - *Ius in bello*, which addresses the way in which a war must be fought.

> ***Ius ad bellum*** refers to criteria for deciding when going to war might be justifiable.
>
> ***Ius in bello*** refers to criteria for deciding how a war, once started, must be fought.

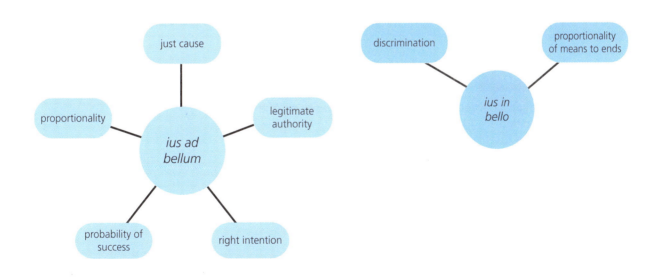

Weapons of mass destruction

- These are sometimes given the acronym of ABC weapons: atomic (nuclear), biological and chemical.
- The effects of exploding a nuclear warhead can be assessed from the dropping of atomic bombs in 1945 on Hiroshima and Nagasaki and from the Chernobyl nuclear power plant explosion in 1986.
  - They include heat, blast and radiation that would prove lethal over a wide geographical area.
  - The environmental damage would last for thousands of years.
- Biological weapons may be sprayed or transmitted through the bites of infected insects or contamination of food and water supplies, with deadly effects.
- Chemical weapons cause injury, disability and death to animals and humans in the vicinity of their use; this has been seen in the civil war in Syria.

Weapons of mass destruction could thus never fulfil the Just War criteria of discrimination, **proportionality** and probability of success.

> **Proportionality** means that expected benefits must be proportional to expected harm and that the means used in war must be proportionate to the ends required.

Christian views on the application of Just War theory to weapons of mass destruction

Opposition	Acceptance
Many Christians view such weapons as intrinsically evil. • Pope Francis has urged the abolition of nuclear weapons, as did the two previous Popes. • Most UK Churches are opposed to the replacement of Trident.	Some argue that modern conventional warfare is almost as bad as ABC warfare in its methods and effects. • Such weapons should be reduced in number by international agreement. • They cannot be un-invented. • It is important to renew Trident as a deterrent. • Fletcher's book *Situation Ethics* implied that the 1945 nuclear attack was the most loving action in that particular situation. He based it on his version of utilitarianism and on his equation of *agape* with justice.

Now test yourself

TESTED ☐

1 What is the difference between the strong and weak versions of the Sanctity of Life principle?
2 What is meant by the Quality of Life principle?
3 From what point, according to the Catechism of the Catholic Church, does the unborn child have an absolute right to respect and protection?
4 Explain what *ius ad bellum* means.
5 Explain what *ius in bello* means.

Dominion and stewardship

Traditionally, there have been two Christian approaches to the environment:

- **Dominion**, which is understood in the sense of humans having power over the rest of the created world.
- **Stewardship**, which involves responsible care for the rest of the created world; humans are God's agents.

The belief that Christians have dominion over animals

REVISED

Traditionally, many Christians have believed and some Christians still do believe that they have virtually unlimited power over animals and the environment.

- This can be seen in the environmental damage caused by the pursuit of wealth at any cost from the time of the Industrial Revolution and on into modern times.
- The pursuit of profit at the cost of terrible suffering to animals can be seen in the practices of intensive farming.
- Read also what the text book and the Ethics revision guide say about animal testing, blood sports, etc.

Many Christians had and still have an anthropocentric view of the universe.

- Aquinas thought that animals were irrational, had no souls and existed solely for the purpose of humanity.
- He opposed being cruel to them, but only because that would encourage humans to be cruel to one another.
- Animals were simply a form of property.

A number of biblical texts can be quoted in support of this:

- In Psalm 8, humans are described as little less than the angels (or possibly, God), with control over all living things.

> **Key quotation**
>
> You made them rulers over the works of your hands; you put everything under their feet: all flocks and herds …
>
> Psalm 8:6–7

- After the Flood, when God made a new covenant with Noah, he said that he gave all animals, fish and plants to Noah for his use.

> **Key quotation**
>
> The fear and dread of you will fall on all the beasts of the earth, and on all the birds in the sky, on every creature that moves along the ground, and on all the fish in the sea; they are given into your hands. Everything that lives and moves about will be food for you. Just as I gave you the green plants, I now give you everything.
>
> Genesis 9:2–3

- For those who take the Noah story as historical fact and literally the word of God, it gives humanity absolute rights over the rest of the created world.
- Referring to humans as created in God's image gives some the anthropomorphic idea that God is actually like humans.

Dominion refers to the power-based approach that some humans take to the environment.

Stewardship is the concept that Christians have a duty of responsible care for the environment.

The role of Christians as stewards of animals and the natural environment

Most Christians today reject the idea of dominion in the sense of a power-based relationship.

They interpret Genesis 1 and Psalm 8 in terms of stewardship.
- They are the guardians of creation, caring for it on behalf of God.
- Their role entails responsibility rather than privilege.

More emphasis is placed on the intrinsic value of animals and the natural environment.
- They point to biblical passages about the goodness and the beauty of creation, for example, in Genesis 1, after each stage of creation, God 'saw and it was good'.

Andrew Linzey sees the created world as **theocentric** (God-centred) rather than anthropocentric.

> **Key quotation**
>
> How many are your works, Lord! In wisdom you made them all; the earth is full of your creatures … There is the sea, vast and spacious … There the ships go to and fro, and Leviathan, which you formed to frolic there.
>
> Psalm 104:24–26

The implications for Christians of the global environmental crisis

Although some people insist that there is no major threat to the survival of our planet as we know it, most people agree that action must be taken to deal with
- the burning of fossil fuels
- many different types of pollution on land, in the oceans and in space.

Pope Francis' encyclical (letter) *Laudato Si* addresses the environmental crisis, rejecting an anthropocentric attitude and urging responsible care.

> **Key quotation**
>
> We are not God. The earth was here before us and it has been given to us. … Although it is true that we Christians have at times incorrectly interpreted the Scriptures, nowadays we must forcefully reject the notion that our being created in God's image and given dominion over the earth justifies absolute domination over other creatures.
>
> *Laudato Si*

- Many churches are being urged to promote **eco-theology** and use eco-friendly practices.
- A Rocha is an international Christian environmental organisation with projects in many different countries.

Theocentric means God-centred. It is the idea that the whole universe expresses the glory of God.

Laudato Si is the encyclical (letter) written by Pope Francis, urging responsible care for the environment.

Eco-theology is an environmental approach creating a right relationship between religion and nature.

> **Now test yourself**
>
>
> 1 What are the two main Christian approaches to the environment?
> 2 Explain what is meant by an anthropocentric view of the universe.
> 3 How does Genesis 1 support the idea that Christians should take care of the environment?
> 4 What did Pope Francis say in his encyclical *Laudato Si*?
> 5 Name a Christian environmental organisation.

Exam practice: AS-level

1 a Explain the Christian belief in justification by faith.   [15 marks]
   b 'Good moral conduct is not important for Christians who believe in
      predestination.' Assess this view.   [15 marks]
2 a Explain why some Christians disagree with embryo research.   [15 marks]
   b 'The Just War theory has no relevance in a world that possesses weapons
      of mass destruction.' Assess this view.   [15 marks]
3 a Explain why some Christians believe that Christians have dominion over animals.   [15 marks]
   b 'The natural environment exists for humans to use as they wish.' Assess this view.   [15 marks]

Exam practice: A-level

1 a Examine the belief of some Christian traditions in justification by faith and works.   [10 marks]
   b 'Good moral conduct is not important for Christians who believe in
      predestination.' Evaluate this claim.   [15 marks]
2 a Examine the influence of belief in the sanctity of life on Christian attitudes to the
      unborn child.   [10 marks]
   b 'The Just War theory has no relevance in a world that possesses weapons
      of mass destruction.' Evaluate this claim.   [15 marks]
3 a Examine how religious teachings influence the attitudes of Christians to animals.   [10 marks]
   b 'The natural environment exists for humans to use as they wish.' Evaluate this claim.   [15 marks]

5 Expressions of religious identity

Baptism

The significance of baptism

REVISED

The word 'baptise' means 'to dip' and in a number of religions, initiation into the faith is marked by pouring water over someone or immersing a person in it. In the twenty-first century, there are three approaches to baptism:

- Many Churches (e.g. Catholic, Anglican, Methodist) practise infant baptism.
  - It is the Catholic rite which will form the focus of study.
- Some Churches (e.g. Baptist, Pentecostal) practise believers' baptism only.
  - The views of Baptists on infant baptism will also be studied.
- Some Churches reject baptism altogether.
  - Quakers and the Salvation Army reject all outward symbols and rituals.
  - They think that being a Christian is all about leading a Christian lifestyle.

Biblical background

- It is not called baptism, but the ritual of being immersed in water was and still is used in Judaism as a sign of cleansing from religious impurity or of being set apart for a particular role.
- Shortly before Jesus began his ministry, John the Baptist was baptising people by total immersion in the River Jordan in preparation for the coming of the Messiah who would inaugurate the Kingdom of God.
- John's baptism symbolised for those who were baptised:
  - their penitence for their sins
  - God's forgiveness of their sins
  - a new start in readiness for the Kingdom.
- Jesus showed his support for John's ministry by coming to be baptised.
  - When he emerged from the water, he had a vision (see the account of this in the section on the Trinity in Chapter 2 of this revision guide).
  - This marked the end of Jesus' former way of life as a carpenter and the start of his ministry.
- Although he may not have baptised people himself, Jesus saw it as a powerful symbol of spiritual rebirth and as a sign of entry into the Kingdom of God.

After his resurrection, he instructed his disciples to baptise converts.
- Baptism therefore became an important **rite of initiation** for converts to Christianity.
  - Sometimes whole households were baptised.

> **Key quotation**
>
> Very truly I tell you, no one can enter the kingdom of God unless they are born of water and the Spirit.
>
> John 3:5
>
> Therefore go and make disciples of all nations, baptizing them in the name of the Father and of the Son and of the Holy Spirit …
>
> Matthew 28:19

> **Rite of initiation** refers to a ceremony that marks becoming a member of a particular group. Baptism confers membership of the Christian community.

Significance of infant baptism in the Catholic Church

Baptism is a sacrament. It effects a real inner change in the baptised person's soul.

Catholics practise infant baptism (**paedobaptism**) for the following reasons:

- It cleanses the child of original sin (see previous chapters in this revision guide for an understanding of this term).
- The water used in baptism is a symbol of God's grace.
- It enables the Holy Spirit to begin the work of transformation in the child's life.
- The child becomes a member of the Christian Church and of the Kingdom of God.
- It is the first **rite of initiation**, opening up the way to the other two rites of initiation (Holy Communion and Confirmation) and to the other four **sacraments**.

There are three aspects to the sacrament:

1 The form in baptism is the anointing of the child, the pouring of water and the words accompanying the pouring of water (see below).
2 The matter in baptism is the use of two blessed oils and blessed water.
3 The intention in baptism is the intention of the priest (or in a life and death situation for the baby, any baptised person) to baptise the child.

> **Key quotation**
>
> Baptism is the way out of the kingdom of death into life, the gateway to the Church, and the beginning of a lasting communion with God.
>
> Youcat 194

Paedobaptism is another term for infant baptism.

Rite of initiation refers to a ceremony that marks becoming a member of a particular group. Baptism confers membership of the Christian community.

Sacrament is an outward and visible sign of an inward and spiritual grace. Catholics and Anglicans regard baptism as a sacrament.

Key rituals of infant baptism in the Catholic Church

Ritual	Meaning
Signing of the cross on child's forehead by priest, parents and godparents	A sign that the child belongs to Christ
Anointing of child on chest with holy oil	A symbol of the strength that baptism gives to fight against all that is wrong
Blessing of the baptismal water	So that the child, through the water, can be 'born of water and the Spirit'
Renunciation of sin and affirmation of faith by parents and godparents	Done on behalf of the child
Dipping the child in the water or pouring water on the child three times, with the spoken words 'I baptise you in the name of the Father and of the Son and of the Holy Spirit'	The central act of baptism, symbolising the washing away of sin, and union with Christ in his death (being immersed in the water) and resurrection (being lifted out of the water)
Anointing the child with the oil of chrism	This seals the child as a member of the Body of Christ and is a sign that the child is chosen for a special task. It is a symbol of the Holy Spirit
Giving a lighted candle to a parent for the child and a special prayer	A sign that the child shares in the risen life of Christ the light of the world and a prayer that the child will be open to hearing the word of God and proclaiming it
Concluding words, the Lord's Prayer and blessing of child, parents and congregation	A reminder of the meaning of baptism and of the parents' duty to ensure the child receives the other two rites of initiation

Significance of baptism in the Baptist Church

REVISED

Baptists refer to baptism as an **ordinance** as they do not believe in the idea of sacraments. The ordinance of baptism is based on Matthew 28:19.

Baptists reject the idea of infant baptism for the following reasons:

- There is no New Testament evidence for it; adults only were baptised.
- Jesus himself was baptised as an adult.
- There is no such thing as original sin, so there is nothing that needs to be removed as soon as possible after birth.
- God's grace is available to all; it is not limited or tied to baptism.
- Baptism is a statement of public commitment to faith in the triune God that is made after careful preparation. It marks becoming a member of the Christian community.

Baptists therefore practise what is known as 'believers' baptism' (**credobaptism**):

- Those being baptised give a public testimony to their faith in Christ.
- They declare their repentance of sin and their acceptance of Jesus as Saviour.
- They are then totally immersed in a baptismal pool, and the minister performing the baptism says, 'I baptise you in the name of the Father and of the Son and of the Holy Spirit'.
- They then rejoin the congregation as full members of the Church community.

Arguments for and against infant baptism

REVISED

For	Against
Baptism is a sacrament that is entirely a gift of God's grace, so even babies can receive it.	Baptism is an ordinance based on the command of Jesus.
Baptism is a sacred mystery: the way it works cannot be understood by humans, so it is not just for those who understand.	Baptism is just a symbol of the believer's desire to start a new life as a member of the Christian community. Only teenagers and adults are able to understand penitence for sin and what they are committing to.
Baptism removes original sin and gives the gift of eternal life, so it should be available to babies.	Baptists reject the doctrine of original sin. Faith, not baptism, is the start of the Christian life.
The story of Jesus welcoming children supports the idea of infant baptism.	Jesus did not baptise the children.
When the New Testament refers to whole households being baptised, this would have included any children.	The households baptised probably referred to all adults, including any slaves.

Key quotation

[Jesus] said to them, 'Let the little children come to me, and do not hinder them, for the kingdom of God belongs to such as these.' [...] And he took the children in his arms, placed his hands on them and blessed them.

Mark 10:14–17

By '**ordinance**', Baptists mean a rule deriving directly from the Bible and particularly from the teaching of Jesus. It is also a ceremony that comes from that rule.

Credobaptism is another term for believers' baptism.

Now test yourself

TESTED

1 Explain what Catholics mean by the word 'sacrament'.
2 Explain what Baptists mean by the word 'ordinance'.
3 Give two reasons why Catholics practise infant baptism.
4 Give two reasons why Baptists do not agree with infant baptism.
5 What words are said in both Catholic and Baptist ceremonies at the moment of baptism?

Now test yourself answers at **www.hoddereducation.co.uk/myrevisionnotes**

Holy Communion

The importance and practice of Holy Communion

REVISED

Most Christian Churches celebrate this community meal, though their beliefs about and understandings of it differ widely.
- For Catholics and Anglicans, it is a sacrament.
- For Protestant Churches, it is an ordinance.
- Quakers and the Salvation Army do not practise it for the same reasons as those given at the start of the section on baptism.

Some of the different names given to Holy Communion

- Holy Communion:
  - 'Holy' refers to the sacred nature of the consecrated bread and wine and of the ceremony as a whole.
  - 'Communion' means 'fellowship'; those sharing the meal enjoy fellowship with one another and with Christ.
- The Eucharist means 'thanksgiving'; at this celebration, Christians thank God for creating the world and for sending his Son as their Saviour.
- The Mass comes from the Latin *Ite, missa est* (Go, you are sent out) and is a reminder to Catholics especially that, fortified with the Body and Blood of Christ, they are able to serve Christ in the world.
- The Lord's Supper links the celebration to the Last Supper, the name given to the last meal Jesus had with his disciples.
- The Breaking of Bread is another symbol of sharing with one another, as the bread is broken and distributed; it symbolises the unity of the community.
- The Divine Liturgy is the name used by the Orthodox Church; it means 'holy work'.

> **Key quotation**
>
> Holy Eucharist is the sacrament in which Jesus Christ gives his Body and Blood – himself – for us, so that we too might give ourselves to him in love and be united with him in Holy Communion. In this way we are joined with the one Body of Christ, the Church.
>
> Youcat 208

Holy Communion in the Catholic Church

REVISED

Practices associated with Holy Communion (Mass)

- In the Eucharistic Prayer, the bread and wine are consecrated; certain ritual actions are performed as the account of the Last Supper from 1 Corinthians is repeated.
- After the Lord's Prayer, the sharing of the peace (shaking hands with one another) and the ritual breaking of the bread (known as the Fraction), Catholics go to the priest to receive Communion.
  - They always receive the bread, but not always the wine.
  - The priest consumes any remaining consecrated elements rather than throwing them away.
- The Mass ends with a blessing from the priest and the words 'Go forth, the Mass is ended'.

> **Key quotation**
>
> The Lord Jesus, on the night he was betrayed, took bread, and when he had given thanks, he broke it and said, 'This is my body, which is for you; do this in remembrance of me.' In the same way, after supper he took the cup, saying, 'This cup is the new covenant in my blood; do this, whenever you drink it, in remembrance of me.'
>
> 1 Corinthians 11:23–25

The importance of Holy Communion (Mass)

Catholics believe in **transubstantiation**.
- This means that when the bread and wine are consecrated, although their physical appearance, taste and texture remain the same, their substance is changed and they become the Body and Blood of Christ.
- Christ is really present in the consecrated bread and wine.

It is a sacrament.
- In receiving Communion, Catholics receive Christ into their bodies.
- This spiritual feeding makes a real change to them.
- Through it they are united with Christ and with one another.
- It is a foretaste of the heavenly Kingdom of God.

There are three aspects of any sacrament; form, matter and intention. In Holy Communion these are:
- Form: the ritual actions and words used at the **consecration**.
- Matter: the bread and wine.
- Intention: the intention of the priest to celebrate Mass.

The Mass is a re-enactment of the sacrifice of Christ on the cross for human sin.
- The **Fraction** symbolises the breaking of Jesus' body on the cross.
- The sharing of the Peace is a sign of the unity of those present with one another.
- At the end of the Mass, Catholics are sent back into their homes and communities to spread to everyone by word and action the love of Christ that they have experienced in the Mass.

> **Transubstantiation** is the name given to what happens when the bread and wine are consecrated: their substance is changed and they become the Body and Blood of Christ.
>
> **Consecration** means 'making holy' and refers to the part of the Eucharistic Prayer when the priest invokes the presence of the Holy Spirit, performs certain ritual actions and repeats the account of the Last Supper.
>
> The **Fraction** refers to the ritual breaking of the consecrated bread as a symbol of the breaking of Jesus' body on the cross.

Holy Communion in the Baptist Church

REVISED

Practices associated with Holy Communion

- There are readings from the Bible and a sermon.
- The holy table is prepared with cubes of bread and individual glasses of grape juice or wine.
- The minister reads out the passage from 1 Corinthians quoted above.
- People pass round the bread and the wine, serving one another.
- Anyone, even young children, may receive Communion. It is for 'those who love the Lord Jesus'.

The importance of Holy Communion

- It is an ordinance. Jesus said, 'Do this in remembrance of me'.
- It is a memorial of the Last Supper and of Jesus' saving death.
- It does not affect any spiritual change in those who receive the bread and wine.
- Its main value is to bring the community together to remember what Jesus did.

The significance of Jesus' actions at the Last Supper

The Last Supper, Luke 22:17–20

Holy Communion originated from the Passover meal that Jesus ate with his disciples in the upper room of a house in Jerusalem on the night before the crucifixion.

- Passover is an annual celebration of the Exodus, the escape of Moses and the Israelites from slavery in Egypt, thanks to the miracle wrought by God in the crossing of the Red Sea. The special Passover foods have symbolic significance linked to the great act of deliverance.
- At the Last Supper, Jesus gave the bread and wine a new significance linked to his death, the bread symbolising his body, and the wine symbolising his blood. The change in symbolism was a sign of the new covenant to be established by Jesus' saving death.
- There are several references in the New Testament to celebrations of Holy Communion and to beliefs about it, so it was an established practice within 20 years of Jesus' death.

> **Key quotation**
>
> [Jesus] took bread, gave thanks and broke it, and gave it to them, saying, 'This is my body given for you; do this in remembrance of me.' In the same way, after supper he took the cup, saying, 'This cup is the new covenant in my blood, which is poured out for you.'
>
> Luke 22:19–20

The significance of repeating Jesus' words and actions from the Last Supper

In the Catholic Church, this is seen as highly symbolic:

- Jesus is referred to as the Paschal (**Passover**) Lamb: his death on the cross was a sacrifice to atone for humanity's sins.
- Like the Passover meal, Holy Communion celebrates deliverance from slavery, but freedom from the slavery of sin rather than from physical slavery.
- Jesus' death, celebrated in Holy Communion, achieved reconciliation between God and humanity.

In the Baptist Church, Holy Communion is just a simple meal to remember what Jesus said and did: symbolism is not important.

The **Passover** is a meal celebrated annually by Jews, which celebrates the liberation of Moses and the Israelites from slavery in Egypt; the Last Supper was, according to the first three Gospels, a Passover meal.

Now test yourself

1. Why do members of the Salvation Army not celebrate Holy Communion?
2. Give two other names that are used for Holy Communion.
3. What words did Jesus say over the bread when he was at the Last Supper?
4. What actions did he perform with the bread?
5. What words did Jesus say over the wine when he was at the Last Supper?

The mission of the Church

Right from the very start of its existence, the Church has been a missionary Church. In his commission to the disciples, Jesus told them to go out into the world to spread the good news in teaching and healing. The New Testament relates how in the early days of the Church's existence, Christians were involved in the three aspects that are still typical of Christian mission in the modern world:

- evangelism
- mission to the Christian community
- mission to the poor and disadvantaged, both in the UK and throughout the world.

Mission as evangelism

Evangelism in the early Church

In less than 30 years after the ministry of Jesus, the story and meaning of his life, death and resurrection had been taken throughout the Mediterranean world.

This **evangelism** was carried out by Jesus' disciples (e.g. Thomas is said to have founded the Church in India) and by other converts, some of whom would have been merchants and traders.

> **Evangelism** is proclaiming the gospel (good news) about Jesus, usually to non-Christians.

Evangelism in the nineteenth century

Evangelism continued throughout the succeeding centuries but took on a new dimension when powerful European nations created empires, creating colonies in the Americas, Africa and Asia.

In nineteenth century Britain, there were a number of societies who sent out trained missionaries to these colonies to convert those who lived there. These missionaries learned the language of the people and lived among them, teaching them about Christianity and also providing medical care and education.

Evangelism in the modern day

In the twentieth century, it was common for local Church communities in the UK to support missionary families financially and in prayer and in return, to receive newsletters about the work going on. The focus now is often less on conversion from other faiths to supporting local Christian communities in outreach projects (such as assisting the clergy of Cairo cathedral in their work with those who seek to survive by recycling rubbish in the city's rubbish dumps).

Some missionaries, supported financially by local UK Church communities, work in secular occupations, e.g. university teaching or nursing, and teaching the gospel to any who wish to hear it.

Throughout the twentieth century in the UK, the numbers of Christians attending churches began to decline and a whole generation had grown up with little connection with religion. So in 1977, the Alpha Course was started in which Christians invited non-churchgoers to a meal, followed by a talk and discussion about aspects of the Christian faith.

Fresh Expressions is a movement that provides alternative forms of Church by going to where people are, rather than expecting people to come into an existing church building. This includes, among many others, churches in pubs, cafés and skate parks.

Mission to the poor and disadvantaged

Mission in the early Church

In the early centuries, the Church was noted for its care of those in need. For instance, when famine broke out in Jerusalem and food prices would have rocketed, the Christians of Antioch in Syria sent money.

Development of the mission of the Church

Over the centuries, charity schools were set up for the poor, financed by bequests from Christians who were well off.

In the nineteenth century, the Church of England Children's Society (now simply known as the Children's Society) was formed to provide homes with a loving family environment for homeless children. The Society still provides care in the form of family day-care centres, giving advice and campaigning for social justice.

In the 1980s, the Church of England set up the Church Urban Fund to address the considerable poverty it had identified in many towns and cities in three ways:
- working in local communities with churches and other organisations to deal with particular issues
- addressing hate and prejudice by encouraging community cohesion and providing a safe place where people can go and discuss their problems over a cup of coffee
- setting up community-based responses and financial services to address the distress caused by unmanageable debt.

From the 1990s and continuing today, practical help has been given to the poor through the setting up of food banks. Churches are often involved in the management of these.

Another area of need relates to the lifestyle of many young people who regularly go clubbing, often drinking heavily, and is addressed by street pastors. These are Christian men and women from local churches who are trained to listen to and help all they come across without being judgemental in any way.

The Society of St Vincent de Paul is a Catholic organisation operating in churches, schools and universities that sees itself as fulfilling Jesus' command in the parable of the sheep and the goats.
- Members are involved in a wide range of work, e.g. repairing and distributing donated furniture, providing debt advice and counselling, teaching literacy and numeracy, providing holidays for disadvantaged families, etc.

The Churches have also been responsible for setting up aid agencies whose main concern is those suffering poverty in LEDCs (less economically developed countries). For instance, the Catholic bishops in the UK set up CAFOD.
- These aid agencies usually work through partner churches and other reliable organisations in the countries where help is needed.
- They provide emergency and long-term development aid, encouraging sustainable and environmentally-friendly practices.
- They campaign for global justice.

> **Key quotation**
>
> Truly I tell you, whatever you did for one of the least of these brothers and sisters of mine, you did for me.
>
> Matthew 25:40

> **Key quotation**
>
> If anyone has material possessions and sees a brother or sister in need but has no pity on them, how can the love of God be in that person?
>
> 1 John 3:17

Mission to the Christian community

- In the nineteenth century, the Industrial Revolution led to thousands of people moving to towns and cities and the Church's missionary focus in the UK was in providing money to build new churches, training clergy and setting up Sunday schools, etc.
- Things changed, however, in the twentieth century, with a rapid decline in church attendance in many denominations. Churches are working to find new ways of providing for the needs of their congregations.
- One exception to this decline is the rapid growth of evangelical charismatic Christianity which has led to the building of many new churches and to more traditional forms of evangelism, e.g. hiring football stadia for crusades and healing services. Often at these, people who are ill or suffering from some kind of disability come to the front for the laying on of hands, and in some cases they claim that they have been healed.
- Evangelical Christians also run Spring Harvest. These are holiday camps that take place in some popular holiday resorts. Children and young people learn more about the Christian faith and engage in a range of activities. Some of these activities are explicitly religious; others focus simply on enjoyment of one another's company in activities such as football.
- There is a growing emphasis on ecumenism, which is the drive to promote unity between the different Christian Churches.
  - During Lent (which is the six weeks before Easter when Christians try to grow closer to Christ), Christians from different denominations may have Bible study or follow a specially devised Lent course in someone's home. In this way, they learn from each other and grow closer together.
  - They often work together in caring for the community. They may run joint day-care centres for those who would otherwise be housebound, or volunteer to help in food banks.
  - In some places, they share buildings for worship. In this way, they learn that what unites them is far greater than what divides them.

Now test yourself

1. What three aspects of mission have been typical of the Christian Church right from the start of its existence?
2. How has the focus of Christian evangelism in today's world changed from nineteenth century evangelism?
3. Why was the Alpha Course set up?
4. Outline the work of Christian street pastors.
5. What is ecumenism?

Exam practice: AS-level

1 a Explain the importance of infant baptism for Catholics. [15 marks]
  b 'A person must be baptised to be a Christian.' Assess this view. [15 marks]
2 a Explain the importance of Holy Communion in Christianity. [15 marks]
  b 'For Catholics, Holy Communion is of central importance to the Christian life.'
    Assess this view. [15 marks]
3 a Explain how and why Christian evangelism changed in the twentieth century. [15 marks]
  b 'The mission of the Church has remained unchanged throughout Christian history.'
    Assess this view. [15 marks]

Exam practice: A-level

1 a Examine why there are different views in Christianity about infant baptism. [10 marks]
  b 'A person must be baptised to be a Christian.' Evaluate this claim. [15 marks]
2 a Examine the importance of Holy Communion in Christianity. [10 marks]
  b 'For Catholics, Holy Communion is of central importance to the Christian life.'
    Evaluate this claim. [15 marks]
3 a Examine different ways in which Christians have continued to fulfil the commission
    that Jesus gave to his disciples after his resurrection from the early twentieth century
    to today. [10 marks]
  b 'The mission of the Church has remained unchanged throughout Christian history.'
    Evaluate this claim. [15 marks]

6 Christianity, gender and sexuality

Historical and social factors that have influenced developments in Christian thinking about women

This is a matter that is currently the subject of hot debate within many of the Christian Churches. There are strong disagreements both between and within them. Views on the role of women within the Church range widely from extreme traditionalist beliefs held by many fundamentalist evangelical Christians to the very liberal approach of the Quakers. Christian thinking is affected by a range of influences:

- What New Testament texts have to say about the role and status of women. Interpretations of these texts are also influenced by attitudes to nineteenth and twentieth century biblical criticism.
- Social attitudes to women, which have changed immensely over the centuries.
- The rights given to women by secular government. Here, the focus will be on UK law.

The role and status of women in the New Testament REVISED

Jesus clearly regarded women highly.
- He taught them in the same way as he taught his disciples, for example, when he ate with Martha and Mary and when he spoke to the Samaritan woman at the well.
- He defended the woman who anointed him during a meal at Bethany for her action and rebuked those who criticised her.

Throughout Jesus' itinerant ministry, he had been accompanied by women as well as by his disciples and they assisted at his burial. But feminists would object to their role as they had cared for his needs; they were not carrying out preaching and ministry as the twelve disciples were, and after his resurrection, Jesus did not commission them as future leaders.

One of the most important statements about human status in the New Testament is found in Paul's letter to the Galatian Christians. In it, he stated explicitly that because all are now 'in Christ', racial, social and gender distinctions do not apply; they have no meaning.

When Paul wrote to the Christians in Rome, he told them to show respect to Phoebe who was a woman deacon, and he commended a number of other women who were fellow workers with Paul and were 'working hard in the Lord'.

However, a negative attitude to women is shown in Paul's first letter to the Christians in Corinth. Taken as it stands, it displays a view that would now be regarded as sexist. There is further consideration of this later in the chapter.

There are two further references made in letters traditionally ascribed to Paul (1 Timothy 2 and Ephesians 5) and both of them are very controversial and are also considered later in this chapter. In Ephesians 5, women are portrayed as subordinate to their husbands and are told to be submissive to their authority.

> **Key quotation**
>
> There is neither Jew nor Gentile, neither slave nor free, nor is there male and female, for you are all one in Christ Jesus.
>
> Galatians 3:28

> **Key quotation**
>
> Women should remain silent in the churches. They are not allowed to speak, but must be in submission, as the law says. If they want to inquire about something, they should ask their own husbands at home; for it is disgraceful for a woman to speak in the church.
>
> 1 Corinthians 14:34–35

Pre-nineteenth century views on women

REVISED

For most of this time, the views held by secular society about women were similar to those held by the Church.

In the early centuries of the Church's existence, some Church leaders held views that were often sexist and sometimes misogynist.
- Tertullian (c. 155–244 CE) referred to women as 'the devil's doorway'.
- Augustine of Hippo and others blamed Eve for the Fall.
- In the fifth century, a number of Church Councils banned women from being ordained as deacons, and the Pope stated his opposition to women's involvement in celebrating the Eucharist. This suggests that women had been acting in leadership roles in some churches.
- The role of women was generally restricted to marriage and motherhood, but the development of the monastic system with its rule of **celibacy** offered an escape from male domination for some. According to Martin Luther, women should 'remain at home, sit still, keep house, and bear and bring up children'.

Some medieval women became highly influential, and have been regarded as early feminists.
- Hildegard of Bingen (twelfth century) was not only in charge of her convent, but was also a respected musician, poet and naturalist whom many medical men consulted about herbs that were useful for healing.
- The writings of Mother Julian of Norwich (fourteenth century) are still in print.

> **Celibacy** refers to the choice to abstain from marriage and sexual relations.

> **Key quotation**
>
> As truly as God is our Father, so truly is God our Mother.
> Julian of Norwich, *Revelations of Divine Love*

Post-nineteenth century views on women

REVISED

- In one respect, little changed at first. Because of the Industrial Revolution, men went out to work and women remained at home to carry out domestic duties and rear the children.
- However, changing ideas about the nature of humankind as endowed with reason encouraged the spread of education, and this included women.
- Women gradually became accepted into professions such as medicine and many of those with money and influence became involved in charitable work.
- Catherine Booth (the wife of the founder of the Salvation Army) claimed that women were particularly suited to public speaking and preaching.
- In the twentieth century, the First World War meant that women played a key role in keeping the country going while the men were fighting. This forced society into a reassessment of their status.
- Gradually women acquired equal employment rights, such as equal pay, though women are still a minority in senior management positions. Additionally, some Christian denominations do not have women in leadership roles.
- Politically, women exercise power, as currently demonstrated by Theresa May and Angela Merkel. There are now far more women MPs than a few decades ago.
- The question for today's Church remains how to respond to social changes. Should they conform to the norms of secular society or should they hold to the traditional interpretation of biblical texts? The rise of biblical criticism during the nineteenth and twentieth centuries contributes to this debate.

The development of biblical criticism

Increasingly over the past two centuries, **liberal theologians** have claimed that the Bible should be studied in the same way as other literature.

This has led to the development of a range of tools of **biblical criticism**: examining the Bible as a whole, the different books that comprise the Bible and analysing the contents and sometimes the individual words in those books. This entails looking at many things including:

- the language in which a text was written, including differences in the early copies of the text. For example, in Mark's account of Jesus healing a man with leprosy, most texts have the Greek word 'filled with compassion', but some early manuscripts have 'filled with anger'.
- literary genres. For example considering whether a given book is a historical account, poetry, early liturgy or a letter.
- an understanding of the cultural views from which a text sprang. For example, considering whether the subordination of wives to husbands found in Ephesians reflects the cultural 'blinkers' of the first century writer rather than God's purpose for marriage.

Liberal biblical criticism would also consider relevant archaeological evidence (or lack of it), extra-biblical written sources, and parallels with other biblical texts and non-biblical literature; for example, comparing the status of men and women according to Genesis 1 with that in the Babylonian creation story, which is thought to be either the source of or a parallel version of Genesis 1.

Negative attitudes to use of biblical criticism

There are two main criticisms levelled at liberal biblical criticism by different theologians:

- Karl Barth rejected the liberal approach. He said that the Bible passes judgement on human reason, not the other way round. The Bible should be allowed to challenge secular values, rather than having its interpretation driven by them. This is the basis of the way many Conservative Evangelical Christians interpret the Bible.
- Many fundamentalist Christians reject anything but a literalist interpretation of the Bible. They believe that the Bible is the infallible word of God, so the role and status of women in the Church is not a matter for debate; it is as set out in 1 Corinthians and 1 Timothy. This would be applied to theological decisions, not only understanding the role of women.

> **Liberal theologians** aim to analyse the Bible and Christian teaching, using modern thought informed by reason and science.
>
> **Biblical criticism** uses the same tools as used in other literature in order to come to a fuller understanding of the Bible. It uses a range of different approaches.

Liberal Christian application of Biblical criticism to 1 Timothy 2:8–15

1 Timothy 2:8–15

> **Key quotation**
>
> Therefore I want the men everywhere to pray, lifting up holy hands without anger or disputing. I also want the women to dress modestly, with decency and propriety, adorning themselves, not with elaborate hairstyles or gold or pearls or expensive clothes, but with good deeds, appropriate for women who profess to worship God. A woman should learn in quietness and full submission. I do not permit a woman to teach or to assume authority over a man; she must be quiet. For Adam was formed first, then Eve. And Adam was not the one deceived; it was the woman who was deceived and became a sinner. But women will be saved through childbearing – if they continue in faith, love and holiness with propriety.
>
> 1 Timothy 2:8–15

Many biblical scholars argue that there was an issue in the Christian community (probably Ephesus) to which 1 Timothy was addressed.

- Ephesus was the most important centre for fertility worship in the region, and many converts would have come from that background; some of the women may have been temple prostitutes in the cult of the mother goddess.
- This is supported by the Greek word translated as 'assume authority'. It is the only time it occurs in the New Testament, and in other Greek literature it does not have that meaning until centuries later. In the time to which 1 Timothy belongs, it had sexual connotations in the sense of someone 'leading someone on'.
- If this was the case, it would explain why the author of the letter wrote as he did.

1 Corinthians 14:34–35

It is possible that 1 Corinthians 14:34–35 are a later addition (a marginal note) to the text, based on 1 Timothy 2:8–15, as a number of early manuscripts omit these verses.

> **Key quotation**
>
> Women should remain silent in the churches. They are not allowed to speak, but must be in submission, as the law says. If they want to inquire about something, they should ask their own husbands at home; for it is disgraceful for a woman to speak in the church.
>
> 1 Corinthians 14:34–35

Catholic view on the ordination of women

The Catholic Church has a **complementarian** approach to the role of women. This is the view that men and women are equal in God's sight but have different roles in life. This approach is supported by Natural Law.

Apostolic Succession can only be passed on from men to men:
- Unbroken succession goes back to Jesus' Apostles, all of whom were men.
- This position was confirmed in 1976 by a Vatican declaration.
- The declaration states that Jesus' radical attitude of great respect for women provides a model to be followed, but that does not entail leadership in the Church, since Jesus chose only men to be Apostles.

> **Key quotation**
>
> The rule that only men may receive Holy Orders in no way demeans women. In God's sight, man and woman have the same dignity, but they have different duties ... The Church sees herself as bound by the fact that Jesus chose *men* exclusively to be present as the Last Supper for the institution of the priesthood. ...
>
> Youcat 257

Protestant views on the role of women in the Church

- Many Protestants believe in the **priesthood of all believers** (see Chapter 4 of this revision guide). They do not believe in ordination to the priesthood since all vocations are of equal value.
- Many Protestants have an **egalitarian** approach. This means that women may hold positions of leadership, just as men may. For example, in the United Reformed Church, women have been ordained since 1917.

Now test yourself

TESTED

1. Give one example of an occasion when Jesus showed respect for women.
2. Give two reasons why feminists would criticise Jesus' treatment of women.
3. What is meant by a complementarian approach to the roles of men and women?
4. Which Christian denomination has a complementarian approach to the roles of men and women?
5. What is meant by an egalitarian approach to the roles of men and women?

Complementarians believe that men and women are equal in status and value but have different roles to play in the Church. These roles complement each other.

Priesthood of all believers refers to the Protestant belief that all humans can have direct contact with God; there is no need for priests as intermediaries.

Egalitarians believe that equality between men and women extends to their roles. Both should have equal roles in the Church.

Debates about female ordination in the Church of England

Views about ordination of women in the Church of England

There has been debate about the ordination of women in the Church of England since 1920.

In 1944, Florence Li Tim-Oi was ordained priest in China because there were insufficient men available who could serve the Anglicans there.

- As soon as the war ended, she handed back her licence and returned to her role as a deaconess.
- But in 1971, when the Synod of Hong Kong and Macao accepted the ordination of women, her status as priest was officially recognised.

In the UK, there were decades of debate, but in 1994 the first ordination of women as priests took place. It is thought that by 2025 there will be as many women priests as male priests.

Again after much debate, the first Church of England bishop (Libby Lane) was consecrated in 2015.

To prevent a split in the Church of England over the issue of the ordination of women, special provision was made for those who could not accept oversight by a female bishop or the ministry of a female priest.

- Christian communities can state that they will have a male priest only to serve in their church.
- Under this system of 'alternative oversight', 'flying bishops' have been appointed to exercise pastoral care for the churches that object to women's ordination.
- They administer Confirmation and ordain priests to serve in those churches.
- There has been an increase in the number of men seeking ordination under this system.

Some priests have felt unable to remain in the Church of England since 1994.

- Many have received ordination in the Catholic Church.
- In 2011, the Ordinariate was set up to allow Anglican priests who were married to become Catholic priests and also to allow whole congregations to become fully Catholic but retain elements of Anglican practice.

Summary of arguments for and against the ordination of women as priests and bishops in the Church of England

> **Exam tip**
>
> In what follows, 'catholic' does not mean the same as 'Catholic'. The lower case use means 'universal', whereas 'Catholic' refers to the denomination.

For	Against
Sometimes one branch of the universal Church must go it alone in order to do what is right. In declaring the Pope infallible, the Catholic Church did not consult other Christians. So in this case, the Church of England was justified in the action taken without seeking the agreement of other Christians.	The decision lacks 'catholic consent', i.e. it has been made without the consent of the universal Church.
Jesus' decision was a pragmatic one. Had he chosen women, his mission would never have taken off. In any case, the role of women was such that they could not just leave their children behind. The choice of men was based on the culture of the time. The ordination of women likewise reflects the culture of today's society.	Jesus challenged many social conventions of his day but chose only men as apostles and leaders of the Church. Religious change should not be dictated by culture. Although inevitably influenced and often enriched by it, it should not be subject to it.
The idea of equality requires an egalitarian interpretation. To refuse women ordination is to regard and treat them as unequal.	Equality of status does not mean interchangeability: a complementarian approach.
There are metaphors in the Bible that compare God to a mother, but it would have led to the danger of syncretism with fertility religions for Jews to refer to God as Mother. There is no longer this danger, and Mother Julian referred to God in this way.	As a 'Father' in God, the bishop represents the Fatherhood of God. The Bible does not refer to God as mother. Ordaining women as bishops overturns the teaching of the Bible.
Gender should have nothing to do with the Apostolic Succession. There is no reason why the ordination of female bishops should break it.	The ordination of women as bishops threatens the Apostolic Succession and therefore the validity of many of the sacraments.
Biblical writers may have been guided or even inspired by God, but God was working through fallible humans who were also products of their culture. Christians today should use the insights of Church leaders today and of psychology, as well as their own religious experience and the tools of biblical criticism to help them discern what are/are not universal truths in the Bible. Galatians 3:28 would be accepted by most Christians as stating a universal truth.	The evangelical wing of the Church of England opposes the ordination of women on biblical grounds. Texts such as 1 Corinthians 14 and 1 Timothy 3 are to be obeyed as the infallible word of God.

Now test yourself

TESTED ☐

1 In what year did the Church of England first ordain women as priests?
2 In what year did the Church of England consecrate the first female bishop?
3 Why did the Church of England set up a system of 'alternative oversight' for those opposed to the ordination of women to the priesthood?
4 Explain the role of 'flying bishops'.
5 Why did the Catholic Church set up the Ordinariate?

A comparison of the significant ideas of Daphne Hampson and Rosemary Radford Ruether

Feminist theology

There are three strands to **feminist theology**, which has developed largely out of secular feminism:

1 The liberal approach that views Christianity's patriarchal beliefs and structures as problematic, since it denies women's fundamental rights to equality with men.

2 The biblical approach that draws upon texts. Biblical scholars who are Christian feminists may in this way ascribe to God qualities typically associated with women, and draw out the importance of women in the Gospels.

3 The radical approach which claims that the Christian story is a (patriarchal) myth and which wishes to speak of God in other, gender-inclusive terms.

Daphne Hampson (b. 1944)

Hampson is a post-Christian theologian. She rejects Christianity on two accounts:

1 It is based on the belief that there was a uniqueness to the person of Christ or a unique resurrection; a revelation in history. Whereas, since the Enlightenment, we have come to think that there could be no such interruptive events and it is difficult to credit that Jesus' relationship to God could be one of a kind.

2 Given that Christianity is rooted in a belief that there has been a revelation in history, Christians necessarily look to the past. But the biblical literature is imbued with patriarchal imagery and suppositions which are thus carried into the present, perpetuating sexism.

Hampson thinks that the way we seek to express God should reflect human awareness of God, for example that there is a power for healing. Thus she will speak of 'that which is God'. She thinks the Christian story a myth from a patriarchal age; a myth which nonetheless has carried people's sense of God, a sense which we must now express otherwise.

Hampson argues that Christians look to literature from a past age, in which a **patriarchal outlook** is taken for granted.

- God seen as transcendent and is described using male metaphors. This casts humanity into a 'female' position and creates gender hierarchy. This then consolidates gender hierarchy in the human situation.
- Father–Son imagery is dominant. There is a lack of imagery depicting women and men as equal adults.
- Given there was no especial revelation in Jesus there is no particular reason to look to him. The evidence is that Jesus treated persons with respect but, (like his contemporaries), he did not begin to see the inbuilt sexism of his society.

Feminist theology has sought to analyse and challenge the Bible and Christian teaching, seeing them as patriarchal.

A **patriarchal outlook** presents religion from a male perspective. God is seen in terms of male power and transcendence, and men are seen as essentially superior to women.

Androgynous combines male with female characteristics.

Rosemary Radford Ruether (b. 1936)

Ruether is, above all, concerned with the biblical message of liberation. The traditional doctrine of atonement with its masculine ideas of power is replaced with a depiction of Jesus as a radical and liberating prophetic figure.

- She points to the Gospel references to him siding with the marginalised in society, the most vulnerable of whom were women.
- The Kingdom of God is not a heavenly state but is to be set up on earth as a sphere where justice prevails for all, including the non-human world.

Like Hampson, Ruether denounces traditional theology as patriarchal and sexist, but she has remained within the Catholic Church. She condemns the patriarchal religious beliefs both of the early and medieval Church and of much modern Catholicism.

- Traditional doctrines of the Incarnation promote the idea of God as a transcendent, male, power-based being.
- She replaces the term God with God/ess to express a freedom from gender.
- Jesus embodied both masculine and feminine aspects of human nature, so can be seen as **androgynous**.

Hampson/Ruether Debate

In a public debate held in London in 1986 and subsequently published: 'Is there a Place for Feminists in a Christian Church?'

- Hampson commented that one could well be religious and feminist. The problem with Christianity however is that it is a 'historical' religion. Reading past literature that is considered inspired propels the past into the present.
- Responding, Ruether claimed that Christianity is rather an eschatological faith, focussed on the future, liberating reign of God. Always reinterpreting itself, it is open to feminist restatement.
- Hampson insisted that Christianity is not simply a political/social message; Christians believe that a particular revelation has occurred in history – an idea not now credible.
- Accusing Hampson of fundamentalism, Ruether commented that she should know that mythological language is symbolic and not to be taken literally.
- Hampson countered that she fully recognised that Christians need not be fundamentalist, but they must necessarily reference this past revelation. If Christianity is simply mythological, why make use of such a sexist vehicle?

Now test yourself

TESTED ☐

1 What three approaches do feminists take to theology?
2 How are both reason and experience integral to Daphne Hampson's thought?
3 What does Rosemary Radford Ruether mean when she says that Jesus can be seen as androgynous?

Different Christian views about celibacy, marriage, homosexuality and transgender issues

Celibacy

REVISED

In biblical times, most Jews married but celibacy was not unknown. However, as far as we know Jesus did not marry and from his lifetime the Christian attitude to celibacy has changed.

- According to Matthew 19:12, celibacy was seen as a choice made to focus on the Kingdom of God. From the early days of the Church, there has been an acceptance of celibacy as a vocation for some Christians.
- In 1 Corinthians, Paul advocated celibacy unless sexual urges proved too strong, in which case the Christian concerned should marry. This concession was because Paul believed that the end of the world was imminent and marriage would be a distraction from preparing for Judgement Day.
- As time went on, it was clear that Paul had been wrong about the imminence of the Second Coming. Later New Testament writings therefore take marriage as a given.
- From the fourth century, the development of monasticism required celibacy.

- It was not until the twelfth century that there was a definitive rule prohibiting marriage for clergy.
- In the Catholic Church, priestly celibacy is seen as a positive offering of oneself to the service of God. However, because of the fall in numbers of those seeking ordination, there has been pressure to permit marriage for priests.
- The Orthodox Church accepts married men as priests, but it is not allowed after ordination and bishops must be celibate.
- In the Anglican and Protestant Churches, clergy are often married. In fact, some Evangelical Protestant Churches oppose celibacy for their clergy on the grounds that it goes against the teaching of 1 Timothy 3:1–7.

Key quotation

Celibacy does not mean 'remaining empty in love, but rather must mean allowing oneself to be overcome by a passion for God.'

Benedict XVI

Marriage

REVISED

In the earliest days of the Church, Christians were expected either to marry or to remain celibate. Marriage became the norm for almost everyone.

Marriage was seen as a sacrament and raising a family was regarded as a vocation.

- This is still the view of the Catholic Church. If couples divorce, they may not remarry because in the eyes of God and the Church they are still married. Only if an annulment is given, can a Catholic 'remarry'.
- Protestant Churches see marriage as an ordinance and not as a sacrament. Divorce and remarriage are therefore accepted, though those who remarry may be expected first to admit their failure and show their intent to live in their new marriage as God would wish.

Western society is very different from what it was even 50 years ago and this challenges some of the traditional views of marriage:

- The idea that an important purpose of marriage is procreation; nowadays marriage is more about a relationship than having children.
- Many marriages are civil ceremonies with no religious element whatsoever.
- Divorce is much more common now and many people may be unwilling to live celibate lives after divorce.
- Same-sex marriage and the adoption of children by same-sex couples are both legally permissible.

Homosexuality

Less than a century ago, those charged with homosexual offences could expect public disgrace and prison sentences. Now it is the expression of **homophobia** that results in prosecution.

> **Homophobia** is fear of homosexuals. It can lead to hate-filled statements and acts of violence.

Society and the law on homosexuality

Until the second half of the twentieth century, social attitudes viewed same-sex relationships as unnatural and to be discouraged.
- The practice of homosexuality, even in private, was illegal and until the early nineteenth century, was punishable by death.
- Gay people often lived in fear of ridicule, assault and public exposure.

In the last 50 years, both UK law and prevailing social attitudes have changed radically, although homophobia is still seen in the words and actions of some individuals and groups.
- In 1967, homosexual acts carried out in private between consenting adults were decriminalised.
- In 2005, laws permitting both civil partnerships and same-sex adoption came into force.
- The 2010 Equality Act made discrimination on the grounds of sexual orientation a crime and this has led to a number of prosecutions.
- In March 2014, the first same-sex marriages took place. These marriages were civil ceremonies; religious bodies were permitted not to perform them if they did not wish to.

Christianity and homosexuality

The changing views of society which have been reflected in the laws of many western countries have posed a considerable challenge to Christianity. The official position of some Churches is clear, but individual members of those Churches do not necessarily agree with those views. One of the key figures pressing for decriminalisation in the mid-twentieth century was the then Archbishop of Canterbury, Geoffrey Fisher.

> **Key quotation**
>
> There is a sacred realm of privacy ... into which the law, generally speaking, must not intrude. This is a principle of the utmost importance for the preservation of human freedom, self-respect, and responsibility.
>
> Geoffrey Fisher, in support of the Wolfenden Report, October 1957

Biblical teaching on homosexuality

There are a number of texts that refer to homosexuality, or particular homosexual practices, as sinful.
- In the Old Testament, homosexuality was said to be an abomination that was punishable by death.
- In the New Testament, Paul twice denounced homosexuality, including it in a list of other 'anti-social' activities.

However, these have been interpreted differently by various scholars and churches in recent decades. Many Christians today would say that the Old Testament laws and Paul's teaching in the New Testament reflect common cultural attitudes of the time that they were written, and as such cannot be directly applied to modern life.

In the Sodom and Gomorrah story (Genesis 19), it has often been assumed that God's destruction of those cities was because homosexual acts were threatened by a group of thugs. However, a careful reading of the story makes it clear that punishment in the form of destruction came more for lack of hospitality than for homosexuality.

Further to this, some claim that David and Jonathan and Ruth and Naomi had same-sex relationships, though in both cases that is debatable.

> **Key quotations**
>
> Do not have sexual relations with a man as one does with a woman; that is detestable.
>
> Leviticus 18:22
>
> Neither the sexually immoral ... nor men who have sex with men nor thieves nor the greedy ... will inherit the kingdom of God.
>
> 1 Corinthians 6:9–10

Contemporary Christian views on homosexuality

To some extent, these are linked to views about the Bible.

- Many Evangelical Protestants believe that the Bible is the directly inspired and infallible word of God. Homosexual orientation and practice are therefore both 'detestable' and incompatible with being a Christian.
- Other Protestant Churches take into account the insights of biblical criticism and of psychology and genetics. They may fully support the changes in the law, and seek to follow the example of Jesus who challenged social and religious injustice, treating all people as having equal value.
- The Catholic Church distinguishes between orientation and practice. It accepts unreservedly those with homosexual inclinations, but expects them to be celibate.
- The Church of England is torn between the liberal and progressive views of many of its members, together with the knowledge that many of its clergy are gay, and the fundamentalist wing in the UK and in other Anglican Churches, notably in Nigeria. The official teaching is that gay relationships fall short of the ideal which is heterosexual marriage, but that homosexuals should be treated with respect. However, clergy in gay relationships should practise celibacy.

Transgender issues

The 2010 Equality Act includes 'gender reassignment' as a 'protected characteristic'.

The Bible says nothing about changing gender, but the early Church strongly condemned those who underwent surgery to modify their sexual identity. Ordination to the priesthood was not permitted for eunuchs.

- Fundamentalist Protestants believe that God alone decides gender. Since he does not make mistakes, any attempt to change it is an act of rebellion against God.
- Liberal Protestants accept transgender people and transgender rights. Many denominations accept transgender people as ministers.
- The Church of England takes the same approach as liberal Protestantism.
  - Since 2000, transgender priests have continued their ministry and transgender men and women are accepted for ordination.
  - Marriage is permitted where one member of the couple is transgender and special naming ceremonies are proposed for transgender members.
- The Catholic Church rejects the idea of changing gender.
  - A report issued in 2000 said that surgery did not change the identity of the person.
  - It might be permissible in extreme cases, but the marriage of transgender people could never be valid.

> **Key quotation**
>
> We affirm God's love and concern for all humanity, but believe that God creates human beings as either male or female.
>
> Evangelical Alliance, *Transexuality*, 2000

Eunuch is a castrated male.

Now test yourself

1 How do Catholics view priestly celibacy?
2 Why do some evangelical Protestant Christians insist on their clergy being married?
3 Explain two ways in which western society challenges traditional Christian views on marriage.
4 What protection has the 2010 Equality Act given to homosexuals?
5 What does the term 'homophobia' mean?

Exam practice: A-level

1 a Examine reasons for the different views held by Christians on the role of women. [10 marks]
  b 'Biblical criticism helps Christians understand biblical teachings about the role and status of women.' Evaluate this claim. [15 marks]
2 a Examine reasons for differing views about female ordination in Christianity. [10 marks]
  b 'Women are highly valued in Christianity today.' Evaluate this claim. [15 marks]
3 a Examine the Christian feminist views of Rosemary Radford Ruether. [10 marks]
  b 'Christian feminism has not had much effect on most Christian communities.' Evaluate this claim. [15 marks]
4 a Examine different Christian views on the issues of homosexuality and changing gender. You should refer to both issues. [10 marks]
  b 'Transgender issues challenge Christian beliefs about God as Creator.' Evaluate this claim. [15 marks]

7 Christianity and science

The emphasis on evidence and reason in science

The rise of science and the scientific method

The Renaissance and Enlightenment periods saw a great change in scientific thinking. It now became a discipline in itself, independent of religious ideas, based on:

- an **empirical approach**: Every scientific hypothesis arose out of evidence that came from experiments or observation
- a **rationalist approach**: The use of reason was needed to interpret the evidence.

These two approaches are integral to science today.

As you will have seen in your study of arguments for the existence of God, there are two distinctive approaches to gaining knowledge:

1 The deductive approach works from the general (a theory) to the specific (the observations).
   If the premises that lead to the conclusion are true, then there is certainty that the theory is true.

2 The inductive approach works from the specific (observations) to the general (a theory).
   The more evidence there is to suggest that the observations are correct, the more likely it is that the theory will be true.
   This approach leads to probability, not absolute certainty.

The inductive approach involves:

- observing and collecting evidence
- coming up with a hypothesis based on examination of the evidence
- repeated testing and maybe modification of the hypothesis
- developing a theory that explains both evidence and results
- using deduction to predict what should be the case and setting up tests to verify or falsify the theory.

> **Empirical approach** refers to an evidence- and observation-based approach.
>
> **Rationalist approach** refers to an approach that uses reasoned thought.

Some Christian responses to the rise of science

REVISED

Deism

Deism was a very popular approach of Christians to science in the eighteenth century age of reason and is still to be found today. It is the belief that a deity (God) 'set things off' (e.g. the Big Bang) and then left the universe to work according to the laws he created it with, but without acting on or influencing it any further.

Most Christians today reject this because it is not compatible with the doctrines commonly accepted by them, such as the Incarnation, the **immanence** of God in prayer and the miracles of Jesus seen in the Gospels.

> **Typical mistake**
>
> The term 'immanence' is an important specialist term relating to the nature of God. It is very important that you spell it correctly. Students often confuse the spelling with another word 'imminence'. If you refer to God as imminent, examiners might think you are referring to Judgement Day.

Immanence relates to God's presence and involvement in the universe. It depicts God's nature as personal.

Existentialism is the view that humans define their own meaning in life; their choices make them what they are.

Existentialism

There is no conflict between religion and science for Christian **existentialists** as the two disciplines are asking different questions about the world. Christian existentialists are concerned with the meaning and purpose of life and view faith as a matter of personal commitment.

> ## Now test yourself
>
> TESTED
>
> 1 What two approaches that developed during the Enlightenment period are integral to modern science?
> 2 What is the difference between a deductive and an inductive approach to gaining knowledge?
> 3 What is the name for the belief that after creating the world, God left it to work on its own with no further involvement from him?
> 4 Why do Christian existentialists think there is no conflict between religion and science?

How scientific explanation has challenged Christian belief

There are a number of major scientific discoveries that have had an impact on Christian beliefs. In this revision guide, we will cover two: Darwin's theory of evolution and the Big Bang Theory.

Darwin's theory of evolution

REVISED

Darwin's voyage on 'The Beagle' from 1831 to 1836 led to him developing this theory.
- His observations during that voyage, for example of the beaks of finches on the Galapagos Islands, convinced him of the truth of natural selection.
- His theory is thus based on inductive reasoning.

Natural selection refers to the way in which individuals better suited to their environment survive to adulthood and reproduce, passing on their characteristics to their offspring.
- Over a long period of time, the characteristics of a species are modified to enable the survival of the species in its environment, as seen in finches on different Galapagos Islands.
- This ultimately leads to the development of new species.
- Those less suited to the environment die out and whole species perish when there are major changes to the environment.
- Darwin referred to this as the survival of the fittest.
- Darwin's theory was highly controversial but it made sense to many people.
- The science of genetics has given further support to his ideas.

> **Key quotation**
>
> One general law, leading to the advancement of all organic beings, namely, multiply, vary, let the strongest live and the weakest die.
>
> Darwin, *On the Origin of Species*

Christian responses to the theory of evolution

REVISED

Darwin's theory certainly challenges traditional Christian views:
- It rejects the idea of all living things being distinct creations.
- It rejects the idea of the essential separateness of humanity from the animal world.
- It suggests that the evolution of species was and is due to random mutations, removing any idea of purpose.

Nineteenth century Christian responses

In the nineteenth century, there were a number of different Christian responses to Darwin's theory.
- Many in the Church of England ridiculed the theory. For example, in a debate in Oxford, Bishop Wilberforce asked T.H. Huxley (who supported Darwin's theory) whether his descent from a monkey came through his grandmother or his grandfather.
- Fundamentalist Christians simply dismissed the theory as human error since it conflicted with the word of God to be found in the Bible.
- Many lost their Christian faith altogether because of the challenge posed by evolutionary theory to traditional views about Genesis and particularly about the concept of humans as created separately in the image of God.
- Most liberal Christians welcomed the theory; they had long rejected any literalist interpretation of the Genesis creation stories. A book (*Lux Mundi*) on the Incarnation incorporated the concept of evolution in its thinking.

Current Christian responses

- Young earth creationists and some old earth creationists (see Chapter 1 of this revision guide) reject Darwin's theory of evolution totally. It is incompatible with the Genesis creation stories, which are the infallible word of God.
- Some old earth creationists accept Darwin's theory of evolution in a diluted form. Evolution explains the development of simpler life forms, but humanity is the result of special creation by God. Humans are not descended from apes.
- Michael Behe's version of Intelligent Design rejects evolution on the grounds of irreducible complexity. At a court trial over teaching creationism, he argued that some complex things like the bacterial flagellum would be unable to work if one part were removed, which means they could not have evolved. Most scientists dismiss his theory as poor science and as creationism in disguise.
- Most Christians reject creationist views on the theory. They see **natural selection** as the way in which God works. Evolution works by the laws of nature and these laws derive from God.
- Catholic teaching rejects creationism as harmful to both science and religion; it sees Christian beliefs and the theory of evolution as compatible.

> **Key quotation**
>
> Theology has no scientific competence, and natural science has no theological competence. ... A Christian can accept the theory of evolution as a helpful explanatory model, provided he does not fall into the heresy of evolutionism, which views man as the random product of biological processes.
>
> Youcat 42

> **Natural selection** is the basic mechanism of evolution: organisms better adapted to their environment tend to survive and reproduce in greater numbers.

Big Bang theory

REVISED

This theory of the origins of the universe developed from observations of the universe as it is now.

- Galaxies are moving away from one another, and the further away they are, the faster they move apart.
- The speed of expansion makes it possible to work out the age of the universe.
- According to this theory, about 13.8 billion years ago, there was a sudden burst of energy that marked the creation of time, space, matter and energy.
- The theory has been supported by the discovery in 1964 of cosmic microwave background radiation and by the abundance of helium and hydrogen in the universe.
- The most widely accepted version of the theory thinks in terms of one event.
- Other versions think in terms of a 'big bang' leading initially to expansion until pulled back by gravity into a 'big crunch', after which it all starts again.
- Some think in terms of multiverses.

Christian responses to the Big Bang theory

There is a range of responses, ranging from the negative (a minority of Christians) to the wholehearted acceptance of it (the majority).

Deism

Deism is the belief that a deity (God) 'set things off' (e.g. the Big Bang) and then left the universe to work according to the laws he created it with, but without acting on or influencing it any further.

The 'God of the gaps' approach

- In the past and still today, some Christians attribute anything they cannot explain scientifically to God, e.g. the idea that directly caused the expansion of the Singularity that led to the Big Bang.
- Science itself shows how flawed this is: as scientific understanding grows, God gets squeezed out of more and more gaps.
- Many Christians see it as diminishing God.

Creationism

- Young earth creationists reject the **Big Bang theory** in all its forms as incompatible with the 6 days creation story in Genesis 1.
- Old earth creationists claim that Genesis 1 is compatible with scientific theory. For example, they argue that the Hebrew word for 'day' can mean an era rather than a period of 24 hours.

The Catholic Church

The Catholic Church fully accepts the Big Bang theory.

Mainstream Christian responses

- The evidence for the Big Bang theory in its most commonly accepted form is very strong.
- It suggests that there was a beginning to the universe, but that demands explanation.
- God is a more likely explanation than chance.

> **Big Bang theory** refers to the theory that the universe began c. 13.8 billion years ago from the rapid expansion of a point of infinite density (a Singularity).

> **Key quote**
>
> The Big Bang, which today we hold to be the origin of the world, does not contradict the intervention of the divine creator but, rather, requires it.
>
> Pope Francis, October 2014

Now test yourself

TESTED ☐

1 On what kind of reasoning was Darwin's theory based?
2 What is meant by 'survival of the fittest'?
3 Give two forms of evidence that support the Big Bang theory.
4 What is meant by the God of the gaps approach?
5 How do young earth and old earth creationists differ in their attitudes to science?

The belief that science is compatible with Christianity

The views of John Polkinghorne

Polkinghorne has written a number of books on the relationship between science and religion. He makes a range of points, and here are a few:

1. Explanation is needed for the fact that the world is intelligible.
   - There is no survival value in the capacity for humans to make sense of the universe. The fact that we *can* suggests that this was part of God's creative plan.
   - Hume suggested that the universe naturally goes through cycles of order and chaos, and that this is a period of order that has nothing to do with God; but for Polkinghorne that is nothing more than speculation.
   - Multiverse theory suggests that the number of universes is potentially infinite, so some of them will appear ordered purely by chance, without the need for God. Polkinghorne insists that here is no evidence that multiverses exist, so the argument against God fails.
   - The **anthropic principle** needs explaining.

2. The idea of providence is at the heart of God's relationship with the world and humankind.
   - God creates, cares for and sustains life for a purpose.
   - God does this in a way that humans cannot detect.
   - Critics would say that this does not really address the evidential form of the problem of evil (see revision guide on Philosophy and Ethics).

3. Both religion and science are concerned with understanding and making sense of experience.
   - Religious experiences do require serious consideration.
   - The differences as seen in the different religions are due to cultural conditioning, but are nevertheless experiences of the same reality.
   - Critics would say that this could lead to the conclusion that the whole of Christianity is simply a culturally conditioned interpretation of religion and its claims cannot be compared or assessed like scientific facts.

4. The Bible gives evidence for Christian claims about Jesus that can be rationally examined just as a scientific theory can.
   - Critics would say that a scientific theory arises out of repeated experiment; claims about Jesus are made on one unrepeatable series of events said to give a unique revelation of God.
   - Scientific theories are empirically based, whereas claims about Jesus are matters of belief.

5. The claim that there is a God seems to many to be one that can be made on the basis of evidence and as such can be treated in the same way as a scientific claim.
   - Christianity is compatible with science, in that both are different ways of understanding reality.
   - Critics would argue that at best this argues for the existence of a God in the sense of deism as opposed to theism. The specific claims about Jesus, which make Christianity the religion that it is, cannot have a scientific basis, but are based on belief.

> **Key quotation**
>
> The rational transparency and beauty of the universe are surely too remarkable to be treated as just happy accidents.
>
> John Polkinghorne, *Questions of Truth: Fifty-One Responses to Questions about God, Science and Belief*

> **Key quotation**
>
> God does not fussily intervene to deliver us from all discomfort but neither is he the impotent beholder of cosmic history. Patiently, subtly, with finite respect for the creation with which he has to deal, he is at work within the flexibility of its process.
>
> John Polkinghorne, *Science and Providence: God's Interaction with the World*

> **Anthropic principle** refers to the incredibly precise fine-tuning of the elements in the universe that are absolutely essential at that particular degree or point for human life to exist.

TESTED

Now test yourself

1 What idea, according to John Polkinghorne, is at the heart of God's relationship with the world and humanity?
2 Why does John Polkinghorne think that Christianity is compatible with science?
3 Give two weaknesses that some people see in John Polkinghorne's claims.

Different Christian responses to issues raised by science: genetic engineering

Ethical issues raised by science

REVISED

Scientific knowledge and technological skills increase at breakneck speed. These often carry ethical implications, particularly in medical science and technology.

Some of the responses to ethical issues raised by science and technology have been examined in the study of normative ethical theories (see the Philosophy and Ethics revision guide) and of key Christian moral principles (see Chapter 4 of this revision guide).

It is clear that views differ widely, even when they are claimed to find a basis in the teaching of the Bible. The problem is that some of today's most pressing issues were not even on the horizon 60 years ago, let alone 2,000 or more years ago.

The increasing understanding of what evolution might mean for humans in terms of progress or regress as a result of environmental change or genetic mutation raises a number of questions:

- In order to improve the human species, should eugenic practices be reintroduced?
- Should genetically modified animals and crops be developed to benefit humans regardless of the potentially negative impact on animals and the rest of the environment?
- To develop a greater understanding of and more effective treatments and cures for cancer, is it morally acceptable to use the genetically modified and patented mouse known as the 'oncomouse'?

The possibilities offered by genetic engineering

Genetic engineering has immense possibilities:

- Treatments for currently incurable diseases such as cystic fibrosis, Alzheimer's disease and Down's syndrome could be developed through genetic engineering.
- It is thought that within a generation, it will be possible for parents to select the DNA that would lead to their offspring being super-intelligent or super-fit (genetic enhancement therapy). These are known as '**transhumans**'.
- Genetically modified animals have produced a human protein in their milk that has been used to treat some people with lung disease.
- Crops genetically modified to produce significantly larger crop yields and to be disease-resistant could help to address the problem of global hunger.

Key quotation

It is entirely possible, given our present increasing pollution of the human gene pool through uncontrolled sexual reproduction, that we might have to replicate healthy people ... Needs are the moral stabilisers, not rights ... If human rights conflict with human needs, let needs prevail.

Joseph Fletcher, *Ethical Aspects of Genetic Control*

Exam tip

You do not need to know in detail the science behind genetic engineering, but just enough for you to understand what follows.

Genetic engineering refers to the attempt to engineer a unique set of genes for the genetic modification of humans, animals and plants. It has a wide range of possible uses.

Transhumans refers to humans who, once the technology has been developed, will have advanced physical, intellectual and psychological powers.

Christian responses to genetic engineering

Catholics and many Protestants hold similar views.

- There is some support for genetically modified crops, given their potential in relation to global hunger, but there is also concern about possibly reducing biodiversity.
- There is some concern about genetic modification of animals among Catholics, as this could be seen as contrary to natural moral law.
- For Catholics and Protestants, there is the practical issue in xenotransplantation (e.g. using the hearts of transgenic pigs) of the transmission of animal diseases to humans.
- **Somatic-cell therapy** is generally encouraged as a responsible use of God-given skills, providing undue risks are not taken and the benefits justify the costs.
- There is much more concern about **germline therapy**, as if a mistake were made, the bad result would be passed down the generations. The bad effects are not necessarily foreseeable.
- **Enhancement therapy**, designed to create a superior human species (transhumans), is rejected by Catholics and many Protestants for many reasons:
  - It would mean that humans would no longer be in God's image.
  - It would promote idolatry.
  - It would lead to children being viewed as a commodity rather than as a gift.
  - It would result in a two-tier society and discrimination based on wealth (i.e. those who could afford the therapy as opposed to those who could not).

Joseph Fletcher, a proponent of Christian situation ethics, however, held very different views.

- He did not advocate an 'anything goes' approach to genetic engineering.
- The proper controls to prevent abuse and exploitation must be in place. But otherwise, although many of the above techniques that are currently available or on the horizon were only a distant possibility in his day, he viewed them positively.
- Rules and principles based on outdated and irrelevant biblical texts or religious dogma should be set aside.
- He foresaw a time in the future when overpopulation or shortage of natural resources would necessitate the genetic modification of humans to enable them to live in the vastly different conditions of space.

> **Key quotation**
>
> Man is a maker and a selector and a designer, and the more rationally contrived and deliberate anything is the more human it is.
>
> Joseph Fletcher, *Ethical Aspects of Genetic Control*

Somatic-cell therapy is a treatment intended to correct genetic disorders (therapeutic genetic engineering). It entails genetic modification of human cells that are not sex-cells and so will affect only the individual being treated.

Germline therapy is intended to correct genetic disorders by genetically modifying the sex cells. This affects not only the person being treated but also his/her descendants.

Enhancement therapy is genetic modification with a social not medical purpose. It is aimed at improving the human race in terms of intelligence, physical strength, appearance, etc.

Now test yourself

1 What is the oncomouse?
2 What are transhumans?
3 How have genetically modified animals been useful in treating people with lung disease?
4 How might genetically modified crops be able to reduce global hunger?
5 What is the difference between somatic-cell therapy and germline therapy?

Exam practice: A-level

1 a Examine how Darwin's theory of evolution influenced nineteenth century
     Christian thought. [10 marks]
   b 'Christianity has no response to Darwin's theory of evolution.' Evaluate this claim. [15 marks]
2 a Examine reasons for John Polkinghorne's belief that science is compatible
     with Christianity. [10 marks]
   b 'Biblical views on creation are totally incompatible with modern scientific thinking.'
     Evaluate this claim. [15 marks]
3 a Examine Christian views on genetic engineering. [10 marks]
   b 'Biblical teachings are totally irrelevant to the issue of genetic engineering.'
     Evaluate this claim. [15 marks]

The challenge of secularisation

Britain as a secular society

REVISED

In pre-Reformation Europe, people's lives and thinking were strongly controlled by the Church. To a certain extent, this continued in Tudor and Stuart England after the Reformation: the monarch dictated the official religion and those who dissented were liable to torture and death.

However, the Reformation encouraged a more individualist approach. By encouraging people to study the Bible and interpret its meaning in the light of conscience, religion became more personal and less of something that was imposed by authority.

- In the eighteenth century, the emphasis on reason, evidence and scientific thought further encouraged a more individualistic approach to religion. It was now possible to be openly atheist or agnostic.
- The nineteenth century laws that permitted greater religious freedom, the horrors of two World Wars in the twentieth century and the challenge to authority experienced in the 1960s decreased further the number of those who attended church and who regarded themselves as 'practising' Christians.
- From the late twentieth century, squabbles and scandals within the Church have led to growing disillusionment with traditional Christianity.

The replacement of religion as the source of truth and moral values

REVISED

Traditionally, ideas of right and wrong were closely linked to religion.
- Many Christians, if asked for the source of morality, would and still do refer to the Bible.
- Right and wrong were and still are seen by many Christians as objectively right and wrong.

However, the development of the social sciences has weakened the notion of objective morality and the links with religion.
- Anthropologists saw concepts of right and wrong as affected by culture.
- Karl Marx regarded religion and its views on morality as a social and political tool wielded by those in power to control the masses.
- Sigmund Freud claimed that it satisfied a psychological need.

Modern **secular humanism** includes the belief that people can live morally good lives without religion.

> **Secular** means concerned with the affairs of this world, so not with religious or spiritual matters.
>
> **Humanism** is the belief that people can lead good lives without holding religious or superstitious beliefs.

Relegation of religion to the personal sphere

Increasing secularisation has meant that faith is seen as an entirely personal choice and a private matter for the individual. People no longer feel that they must declare allegiance to Christianity as Britain's traditional and national religion.

However, Christianity still plays a significant role in Britain.
- The Church of England is the established Church in England and in Scotland it is the Church of Scotland.
- The National Anthem, sung on a wide range of occasions with great gusto, is essentially religious; its opening word is 'God'.

> **Now test yourself**
>
> 1 What in the eighteenth century encouraged a more individualistic approach to religion?
> 2 What has caused the disillusionment with traditional religion that is felt by many people in Britain today?
> 3 Which Christian denomination is the established Church in England?
>
> TESTED

Now test yourself answers at www.hoddereducation.co.uk/myrevisionnotes

Responses to materialistic secular values

The value of wealth and possessions

Materialism is a key feature of modern secular lifestyle, but its roots lie in the sixteenth century. It is also seen as being in absolute opposition to the values of Christianity, but modern Christian attitudes to wealth and possessions are complex.

The growth of materialism

- Post-Reformation views on the value of family life led to a reassessment of attitudes to wealth and possessions: secure family life depended on possessing worldly goods and enough money to pay for them.
- The expansion of Britain's power in Africa, the Americas and the Far East created trading opportunities that led to the development of **capitalism**.
- Capitalism was reinforced in the nineteenth century by the Industrial Revolution. Great wealth was created in banking, businesses and trading. This led to terrible financial poverty and appalling living conditions for those families who flocked to towns and cities to work in factories, etc. This inequality was challenged by the ideology of **communism** promoted by Karl Marx, but it went unheeded by British society as a whole.
- Materialism is now seen at every level of British society:
  - Those who are wealthy tend to see their continued well-being as dependent on acquiring even greater wealth.
  - Those who are poor see the acquisition of money and possessions as the key to happiness.
  - Material possessions are seen as more important than spiritual qualities.

New Testament attitudes to wealth and possessions

In the time of Jesus, wealth was regarded as a good thing, as it was a sign of God's approval. This explains the bewilderment of Peter when in response to Jesus' comment about it being hard for the wealthy to enter the Kingdom of God, he said, 'Then who can be saved?'

Jesus' teaching challenged this.
- He told the rich man that if he wished to gain eternal life, he must give everything he had to the poor (Mark 10:17–22).
- His parable of the rich man and Lazarus (Luke 16:19–31) contained a warning of dire consequences for those who enjoyed great wealth but ignored the needs of the poor. In that parable the rich man was reminded that caring for the needs of the poor was at the heart of the Law and prophetic teachings.
- Jesus did not condemn wealth in itself. Zacchaeus would still have been wealthy even after giving away great amounts of money but Jesus said that he was 'saved' (Luke 19:1–10). Unlike the rich man in Mark's Gospel who could not do as Jesus asked, Zacchaeus was not 'tied' to his wealth.

The rest of the New Testament adopts a similar attitude.
- In the very early days of Christianity, people shared everything.
- When there was famine in Jerusalem, Christians in Syria collected money to send to those in need.
- The possession of wealth was not seen as wrong in itself; it was the attitude to it that mattered.

> **Materialism** is a world view that regards material possessions, wealth and personal comfort as more important than any spiritual beliefs or practices.
>
> **Capitalism** refers to the political and economic system that allows wealth to be controlled by individuals and businesses for private profit.
>
> **Communism** refers to a political system in which power, wealth and status are equally shared by all who live in the community or nation.

Key quotation

For the love of money is a root of all kinds of evil.

1 Timothy 6:10

The relationship between Christian belief and wealth in modern society

A minority of Christians have adopted for themselves the teachings and practices of Jesus and the early Christian Church, setting up communities that mirror the life of the early Jerusalem community.

- The **Bruderhof** was set up in the early twentieth century and its communities are now found in a number of countries, including three in the UK.
- Members of the Bruderhof see materialism as one of the main reasons for the problems facing the world today.
- They live in communities, without any personal property.
- They make certain vows, one of which is to live simply.

At the other extreme of Christian attitudes to materialism is what is known as 'prosperity theology' or 'the **prosperity Gospel**'.

- This thinking developed in the mid-twentieth century in the United States within the Pentecostal tradition and is now an international movement.
- Despite various scandals implicating some of their leaders, many churches have been set up, attracting thousands of adherents.
- It teaches that Christian beliefs and practices will be rewarded by God in terms of material prosperity and physical well-being.
- Members are expected to give generously to evangelistic work and some churches are also involved in social projects.

Mainstream Christian denominations denounce prosperity theology but they do not adopt the Bruderhof approach to wealth. They think that there is nothing intrinsically wrong in having wealth but possession of it entails great responsibilities for its use.

- This follows the example set by nineteenth century Christian industrialists, such as George and Richard Cadbury, who built good housing for their employees, also paying reasonable wages, running a pension scheme and providing medical care.
- Christians are to be responsible stewards of their wealth, sharing it generously and sacrificially with those in need.
- Many churches are involved in the running of food banks and encourage their members to become involved in projects that care for the homeless.
- Some of the voluntary aid agencies working to end global poverty have a Christian foundation, e.g. Christian Aid, Tearfund and CAFOD.

> **Key quotation**
>
> We pledge to give up all property and to live simply, in complete freedom from all possessions.
>
> Bruderhof vow

Bruderhof is an evangelical Christian movement whose members live in communities, having given up all personal property.

The **prosperity Gospel** is a form of evangelical Christianity that views wealth, power and status as rewards from God for strong faith and good works.

Now test yourself

1 What is the world view of materialism?
2 What warning does Jesus' parable of the rich man and Lazarus contain for Christians?
3 How did Zacchaeus' attitude to money differ from that of the rich man who could not do as Jesus asked?
4 What vow do members of Bruderhof communities make?
5 What do mainstream Christian denominations think about wealth?

The rise of militant atheism: the view that religion is irrational

Militant atheism

REVISED

Militant atheism really came into its own in the late twentieth century with the writings of and interviews given by people such as Peter Atkins, Richard Dawkins, Christopher Hitchens and Stephen Fry. These people come from different academic disciplines, but all agree that religion is a dangerous phenomenon that should be annihilated on the grounds that it is irrational and shows a lack of intelligence.

Richard Dawkins: *The God Delusion*

Richard Dawkins is an evolutionary biologist who has a real passion for science, which he communicates in his lectures and his writings. His attacks on religion, however, have created much controversy, as much among scientists as theologians. Michael Ruse, a professor of the history and philosophy of science, said that *The God Delusion* made him embarrassed to be an atheist.

Dawkins attacks religion in a number of ways:
- The God hypothesis (belief in a supernatural being, miracles, life after death, etc.) is **irrational** and contrary to good science.
- Religion is primitive, harmful and has spread like a virus.
- Religion encourages discrimination and is a major cause of conflict.
- Teaching children religion, whether in the home, church or school, is a form of mental abuse that threatens their development.
- People can be morally good without religion.

> **Militant atheism** refers to the view that all religion is a bad thing that must be actively fought against.
>
> **Irrational** means 'without reason', often in the sense of being contrary to reason.
>
> **Magisteria** refers to sources of authority.

McGrath's defence of Christianity: *The Dawkins Delusion*

REVISED

Alister McGrath was an atheist, but became a Christian while studying chemistry at Oxford University. He has expertise in both science and theology. *The Dawkins Delusion* is not an attempt to prove that Christianity is true but seeks to show that Dawkins' arguments are fundamentally flawed. The following are some of the points made in his book.
- He claims that Dawkins is wrong in his assumption that good science is bound to result in atheism. McGrath cites examples such as Francis Collins (the director of the Human Genome project and a Christian) to prove his point
- He challenges Dawkins' view that science disproves religion by discussing the relationship between the two. He claims that religion and science are 'partially overlapping **magisteria**'; they come at the world from two different but equally valid perspectives, which sometimes intertwine and can be mutually enriching.
- He criticises Dawkins for his assumption that all Christians adopt views of God and the Bible which are in fact held only by a minority who are fundamentalist. This shows a very limited understanding of Christianity.
- He accuses Dawkins of fundamentalism in his unquestioning acceptance of some atheist views. Dawkins is biased in supporting evidence that agrees with his position. This is a very unscientific approach.

Now test yourself

1 How is militant atheism different from ordinary atheism?
2 Explain two challenges made to Christianity by Richard Dawkins in *The God Delusion*.
3 Explain how Alister McGrath responds to each of the two challenges that you have selected in *The Dawkins Delusion*.

TESTED

Emergence of new forms of Christian expression

Responses to militant atheism are reactive. Twenty-first century Christianity in the UK is, however, also proactive in the secular world. This can be seen in a variety of ways.

Fresh Expressions

This movement was set up in the Church of England as the result of a 2004 report, and has now been adopted by other Churches. It takes many forms but they are all linked through a central support team.

- The movement has an evangelical aim in seeking to share Christian thinking, but it is not aimed at drawing people into traditional Church communities (though that might sometimes happen).
- It works alongside traditional Churches, not replacing but supplementing them.
- It shares with those who have no contact with Church communities what it means to live in a secular society, so it starts from where people are.
- It is about listening to the life experiences of ordinary people in their everyday situation and considering how the life and attitudes of Jesus might give meaning to those experiences, rather than preaching traditional beliefs and ritual practices.

> **Key quotations**
>
> A Fresh Expression is a form of church for our changing culture established primarily for the benefit of people who are not yet members of any church.
>
> Bishop Steven Croft

The House Church movement

This movement views secularisation as largely hostile to the Church and sees a parallel in the circumstances of Christianity in the first three centuries of its existence, when it suffered persecution by state authorities and by Roman society generally.

- In those early days of the Church, Christians met in private houses.
- The House Church movement seeks to replicate this practice.

The House Church movement is a movement away from meeting in conventional church buildings with all the formality of worship associated with them and is found within most denominations, but is especially typical of evangelical and charismatic traditions. House Churches also have the following features:

- The approach to the Bible is often fundamentalist.
- Those who belong to House Churches focus on their individual experience of God calling them to a particular lifestyle or form of worship.
- The House Church movement has had a tendency to split. From one such split, the British New Church Movement developed. This is a **charismatic** movement modelled on the type of worship practised in some early Christian communities: **prophecy**, **glossolalia**, healing, etc.

> **Charismatic** refers to practices or worship that are believed to be directly inspired by the Holy Spirit.
>
> **Prophecy** in charismatic worship is the Spirit-inspired declaration of God's purpose.
>
> **Glossolalia** is the gift given by the Holy Spirit to people, enabling them to utter sounds and words that are unintelligible to others, but which express a deep devotion and closeness to God. The person is in a trance-like state.

> **Now test yourself**
>
>
> 1 Describe the Fresh Expressions movement.
> 2 What approach to the Bible do many House Church movements take?
> 3 In what ways is the worship of the British New Church Movement similar to that of some early Christian communities?

Emphasis on the social relevance of Christianity

Christianity's continuing relevance to a secular society

REVISED

To some extent, despite declining numbers of regular worshippers, it can be claimed that British society itself still views religion as socially relevant.

- In times of major disasters, people often turn to the Church to express their grief, find comfort and perhaps make some sense of it.
- More locally, the Church often plays a significant part in helping local communities come to terms with a tragedy such as the murder of a child.

Social involvement demonstrates how the teachings of Christianity are socially and politically relevant in the modern world.

- Jesus himself put caring for those in need before religious rules, and Christians today reflect Jesus' teaching in their belief that the Church is the Body of Christ on earth.
- It has a theological basis in a doctrine of the Incarnation: in Jesus, God is immanent and fully involved in the world.

Liberationist approaches: supporting the poor and defending the oppressed

REVISED

Central and Southern America

In the late twentieth century, the extreme poverty caused by political corruption and suppression of any attempt to seek justice elicited two approaches to the problem.

1 Some leaders of the Catholic Church, including the Pope at that time, advocated a non-confrontational and non-violent response.
2 Other leaders of the Catholic Church joined forces with secular protest groups in order to force change. This became known as the **liberationist approach**.
   - Some saw violent action as the only way of removing corruption and establishing justice for the poor.
   - Archbishop Oscar Romero denounced the government's oppression of the poor and violation of human rights in El Salvador, which led to his assassination in 1980. The resulting global publicity raised international awareness of the situation in El Salvador and of the Church's denunciation of it.
   - These aims can be summed up in the phrase '**the preferential option for the poor**', which was at the heart of Jesus' ministry and endorsed by leaders in the early Church.

> **Liberationist approaches** start by analysing the situation of the poor and oppressed and then use the gospel to challenge the causes of their poverty and oppression.
>
> **The preferential option for the poor** refers to Catholic teaching on social justice; it is about giving the marginalised in society the justice that is due to them. Meeting their needs is an absolute priority in Christian living.

Britain

In the late twentieth century, several reports showing high levels of poverty and deprivation were published, including 'Faith in the City' by the Church of England.

As a result of 'Faith in the City', the Church of England set up the Church Urban Fund, which gave grants to both secular and religious organisations to tackle the problem.

Christians of all denominations continue to take responsibility for the secular well-being of society in a range of ways including food banks, day centres for the housebound and provision of hot meals, clothing, and so on for the homeless.

Now test yourself

TESTED ☐

1 Give two reasons why it might be claimed that British society still sees Christianity as socially relevant.
2 How did Oscar Romero display a liberationist approach?
3 What is meant by 'the preferential option for the poor'?

Exam practice: A-level

1 a Examine how secularisation has affected attitudes to religion. [10 marks]
  b 'Christianity will only survive in the modern world if it adopts secular values.' Evaluate this claim. [15 marks]
2 a Examine how Christian teaching influences attitudes to wealth in modern society. [10 marks]
  b 'Christian attitudes to wealth are naive.' Evaluate this claim. [15 marks]
3 a Examine the challenge of militant atheism to Christian belief. [10 marks]
  b Militant atheist views on religion are fundamentally flawed.' Evaluate this claim. [15 marks]
4 a Examine different ways in which Christianity has responded proactively to the challenges posed by secularisation. [10 marks]
  b 'The House Church movement undervalues traditional forms of Christian expression.' Evaluate this claim. [15 marks]
5 a Examine liberationist responses to the problem of poverty. [10 marks]
  b 'The Church should focus on religious matters and leave caring for the poor to the government.' Evaluate this claim. [15 marks]

9 Christianity, migration and religious pluralism

How migration has created multicultural societies which include Christianity

How migration has created multicultural societies

British society has contained communities of people from other cultures for a long time in its history. There were Jewish communities in Britain before their expulsion in 1290 and after their return from 1656. As Britain's overseas trade expanded in the seventeenth century, Muslim communities from the Middle East and Far East settled, mainly in ports such as Cardiff and South Shields. However, **multiculturalism** and **religious diversity** became a recognised feature of British society only from the late twentieth century.

An outline of migration to Britain

- Many people **migrated** from Eastern Europe after the Second World War.
- Many Indians and Pakistanis migrated after Indian Independence was declared in 1947. They continued to come to the UK, peaking in 1972 with their expulsion from Uganda by Idi Amin.
- In the 1950s, there was a severe shortage of labour in the UK, so the British Government encouraged immigration from the Caribbean and Hong Kong.
- In the 1980s, many Somalis came to escape the civil war in their homeland.
- In the 1990s, the Balkan conflict led to many people migrating from there.
- Immigration has continued in the twenty-first century as a result of several factors:
  - the expansion of the EU
  - migrants crossing into Europe from North Africa
  - refugees from the civil war in Syria.

Responses to multiculturalism in the past

Some viewed immigration as a threat to traditional British values, which they linked to Christianity even if they had no real connections with any church.

- Emotive and inflammatory language was used, such as talk of 'being swamped' and Enoch Powell's speech in 1968, warning of disastrous results.
- In modern times, this feeling has been encouraged by some political parties.

Most people saw multiculturalism as an opportunity for enrichment.

- There was a desire to respect and protect all cultures.
- It was seen as a way of promoting tolerance and equal opportunities in all aspects of British life.

> **Multiculturalism** refers to the presence of, or support for the presence of, several distinct cultural or ethnic groups within a society.
>
> **Religious diversity** refers to the fact that there are significant differences in religious beliefs and practices within a society.
>
> **Migration** refers to the movement of large numbers of people from one place to another.

Diversity of faiths in Britain today

REVISED

The 2011 Census showed the following:
- A continuing decline in numbers of those declaring they were Christian (now just over 59 per cent);
- A rise in those of no religion (just over 25 per cent) and in Muslims (almost 5 per cent);
- Statistics for Hinduism, Sikhism, Judaism and Buddhism also showed an increase.

This diversity is not seen in all parts of Britain.
- Some areas of Britain are still monocultural as when people first migrated, they tended to settle in groups and in places where employment was to be readily found.
- Some, for example the Indian Asians expelled from Uganda, were settled in places where local governments said they had the capacity to receive them.

Freedom of religion as a human right in European law

REVISED

The European Convention on Human Rights adopted as law Article 18 of the Universal Declaration of Human Rights.

> **Key quotation**
>
> Everyone has the right to freedom of thought, conscience and religion; this right includes freedom to change his religion or belief and freedom, either alone or in community with others and in public or private, to manifest his religion or belief, in worship, teaching, practice and observance.
>
> Freedom to manifest one's religion or beliefs shall be subject only to such limitations as are prescribed by law and are necessary in a democratic society in the interests of public safety, for the protection of public order, health or morals, or for the protection of the rights and freedoms of others.
>
> European Convention on Human Rights Article 9

This is also a part of British law within the 1988 Human Rights Act. It allows **religious pluralism** by making illegal any attempt to ban or restrict the practice of religion.

Religious pluralism refers to a situation where people of different faiths live in the same society as one another without conflict and show respect to one another.

Religious pluralism as a feature of modern secular states and its influence on Christian thought

As a **secular state**, Britain's population contains many different faiths and many different cultures. It is a society in which there is, to an extent, religious pluralism. A society in which religious pluralism is embraced is characterised by:

- exploring one another's traditions
- helping one another and respecting differences.

There are, however, many criticisms of multiculturalism and religious pluralism:

- Multiculturalism threatens **social cohesion** as there is no sense of a common identity.
- Immigrant cultures might flourish without being **assimilated**, which can lead to a sense of isolation, or discrimination.
- Certain practices carried out by some communities are illegal under British law and cause tensions. For example, female genital mutilation and forced marriages.
- Multiculturalism assumes that no culture can claim to be the best, but a major reason for belonging to a particular religion is the conviction that it offers the best way of life.
- Religious pluralism might work with different practices but there is a real problem when it comes to different beliefs. The existence of statements of belief may make it impossible for someone to accept that the teachings of two or more religions are true at the same time.

> **Secular state** is a country where the government, legal system and society are independent of the teachings of a religion.
>
> **Social cohesion** refers to a situation where different cultures work together, forging a national identity.
>
> **Assimilated** describes when one culture or religious system is totally absorbed by another, losing its distinctive identity.

Now test yourself

1 Give two reasons for twenty-first century immigration into the UK.
2 Why are some areas of the UK still monocultural?
3 Why do many people support multiculturalism?
4 Why do many people support religious pluralism?
5 Give two reasons why some people oppose multiculturalism and religious pluralism.

Christian attitudes to other faiths

Exclusivism

Exclusivism in Christianity claims that Christianity (or one version of it) is the only true faith.

Many verses in the Bible support an exclusivist view of Christianity.

Taken at face value, John 14:6 seems to say that salvation depends on absolute and explicit commitment to Jesus: truth is to be found exclusively in his teaching and way of life.

Some exclusivists make exceptions:
- Children who die before they are able to make this commitment can be saved. This is also reflected in the reason that used to be given for the practice of **emergency baptisms**.
- Those who die never having heard about Jesus will be judged on the conformity of their lives with the natural moral law that some Christians think is built into the fabric of the universe and accessible to all.

Fundamentalists, however, tend to adopt a narrower interpretation of the verse.
- Salvation depends on declared belief in Christ, which means that **evangelism** is an absolute priority.
- Other New Testament texts are quoted as support for their view.
- The belief that God was uniquely revealed in Christ is seen as a central truth of Christianity that is threatened by any dilution of exclusivism.
- Before Vatican II, the official view of the Catholic Church was that there is no salvation outside the Church.
  - That was modified at Vatican II, inspired by Pope John XXIII's observation that 'what unites us is much greater than what divides us'.
  - The 1995 encyclical of Pope John Paul II on Christian unity (*Ut unum sint*) displays a positive and inclusivist attitude to other Christian denominations.

Criticisms of exclusivism
- It limits God's unconditional love and forgiveness by tying him to a fundamentalist interpretation of certain biblical texts.
- It lacks balance.
  - This interpretation conflicts with the teaching of Jesus recorded in Luke's Gospel in particular and with the unconditional friendship he showed to those who were generally despised by Jewish society.
- This conflict points to the fact that the New Testament is a product of the Church.
  - The Gospels were written by those who were members of Christian communities and who had absorbed the outlook and teachings of those communities.
  - John's Gospel is thought to have been written in the late first century and to contain its author's beliefs about the significance for Christian belief of the portrayal of Jesus in the earlier Gospels rather than always reporting what Jesus actually said.

> **Key quotations**
>
> Jesus answered, 'I am the way and the truth and the life. No one comes to the Father except through me'.
>
> John 14:6
>
> Salvation is found in no one else, for there is no other name under heaven given to mankind by which we must be saved.
>
> Acts 4:12

Exclusivism is the view that one religion alone is the only true one.

Emergency baptism refers to baptising those likely to die; it used to be believed that baptism was essential for salvation.

Evangelism refers to spreading Christianity by preaching or personal witness.

Inclusivism

Inclusivism in Christianity says that other religions (or Christian denominations) may have aspects of belief that are the same or compatible with Christianity (or the 'true' denomination) and are therefore themselves 'true'.

- Closed inclusivism takes the approach that one religion does contain all truth, but that other religions have some aspects of it.
- Open inclusivism adopts the approach that one religion has a better grasp of the truth than others, but not all aspects, so it can learn from others.

> **Exam tip**
>
> Before revising the views of Barth and Rahner, it might help to look again at the section on justification in Chapter 4 of this revision guide.

Inclusivism can be interpreted in a number of ways.

- The approach taken by the author of **Luke/Acts** and by Paul in his letter to the Christians in Rome stresses God showing no favouritism.
  - ○ Salvation is open to all.
  - ○ It is based on people's adherence to or rejection of the natural sense of morality that is an inbuilt feature of the world.
- Barth's view is based on his belief that all human nature has been so corrupted by the Fall that everyone, regardless of religion, is totally dependent for salvation on God's grace.
- The Catholic theologian Karl Rahner developed the idea of **'anonymous' Christians**.

Karl Rahner's concept of 'anonymous' Christians

- This is an attempt to reflect the inclusive teaching and lifestyle of Jesus, as seen in the Gospels.
- It sees God's power as transcending human limitations caused by ignorance, error and evil inclinations.
- God's grace is at work in all people; it is not limited to Christians.
- Non-Christians may be saved through good moral conduct, which is not dependent on belief in Christ. This is reminiscent of the belief in justification by works.
- Rahner's view is that non-Christian religions have much in common with Christianity.

Rahner's concept has been criticised from two perspectives.

- Fundamentalists have condemned its inclusivist approach.
- Some liberal Christians, notably John Hick, have accused it of paternalism.
  - ○ It is insulting to other faiths, which should be respected in their own right and not in terms of what they have in common with Christianity.
  - ○ Hick claimed that Rahner's view implied that other religions are flawed.

Inclusivism is the view that although one religion is true, other religions may show aspects of that one true religion.

Luke/Acts are two books in the New Testament that are believed by most Christians to have been written by the same person. So when referring to the Acts of the Apostles, it is customary to refer to 'the author of Luke/Acts'.

Anonymous Christians refers to Karl Rahner's view that non-Christians are able to experience grace and salvation.

How Christian denominations view one another

REVISED

There has never been uniformity in the Church.
- The Acts of the Apostles and Paul's letters show that even in the early days there were disagreements.
- Before what is known as the Great Schism in 1054, when the Orthodox Churches split from the Western Church (which became known as the Catholic Church), there were many councils of bishops to try and deal with disagreements.
- Since the Reformation, there have continued to be further splits and tensions.
- Disagreements relate to a range of issues such as leadership, the authority and interpretation of the Bible, Church organisation, forms of worship and lifestyle.

The Catholic Church

The following are at the heart of the Church's self-understanding:
- The Apostolic Succession is the means of continuity with the teaching of Jesus' Apostles as the Church passes on their teaching in the Apostolic Tradition.
- The Sacraments are the gifts bestowed on the Church as an act of divine grace.

In their relationships with non-Catholic Christians, liberal Catholics adopt the approach of closed inclusivism:
- Other denominations reflect aspects of the Christian faith.
- Only the Catholic Church, however, has true continuity and authority.
- Dialogue is encouraged with non-Catholics, but not compromise.

Protestant evangelical Churches

Protestant evangelical Churches tend to adopt an exclusivist position, based on the primacy of faith.
- Salvation comes by the grace of God through faith, which is a personal commitment to Christ as saviour.

- The threefold ministry of the Church and the sacraments are viewed as unbiblical and so the Catholic, Orthodox and Anglican Churches are in error.
- Those who do not make this personal commitment to God have rejected God's offer of salvation.

The Church of England

The position of the Church of England is more difficult to pin down as it includes members with a wide range of views. It could be said to be inclusivist for the following reasons:
- Its ability, despite all the tensions, to hold together Christians varying widely in outlook, through discussion and a willingness to compromise on non-essentials.
- Its recognition of other Churches, despite differences in structures, etc.
- Its unwillingness to exclude other Christians from the possibility of salvation.

The ecumenical movement

This is a movement aimed at promoting Christian unity.
- In the UK, there is an annual Week of Prayer for Christian Unity led in January.
- In 1948, the World Council of Churches was set up, which seeks to promote dialogue between the member Churches and a greater shared understanding of the Christian faith. The Catholic Church is not a member but it does have representations at its Assemblies, which are held every six to eight years.

> **Ecumenical movement** is a movement aimed at fostering relationships between Christian denominations and promoting unity.

Now test yourself

TESTED

1 Explain what is meant by exclusivism.
2 How could the pre-Vatican II Catholic view of salvation be summed up?
3 What statement by Pope John XXIII encouraged a modification of the official Catholic Church's view on salvation?
4 What attribute traditionally ascribed to God is limited by exclusivism?

Pluralism with reference to John Hick

Hick's view of the nature of God and religion

REVISED

John Hick was in his younger days a conservative evangelical, but gradually moved away from that position to religious pluralism. His starting point on pluralism is his view that the religion of an individual is almost always an accident of birth.

- The relationship between humans and what he thought of as ultimate reality is shaped by history and culture.
- It is a mistake to understand salvation in terms of the sacred writings of one particular religion and to adopt an exclusivist position.
- He rejected the concept of hell as incompatible with belief in an omnibenevolent God.
- Hick distinguished between the concept of ultimate reality and the widely differing views that humans have of that reality.
- He thought that religion was about self-transformation rather than about believing certain teachings and practices are true. This means that differences and so-called incompatibilities between religions are insignificant.

> **Universalism** is the view promoted by John Hick that all humans will be saved by God.
>
> **Interfaith relations** refer to relationships between different faiths.
>
> **Interdenominational relations** refer to relationships between different Christian Churches.

Hick's universalism

- Hick viewed the purpose of human life as one of soul-making or spiritual growth.
- That raised the question of those who died without having fulfilled their purpose and in some cases, having wreaked misery on the earth.
- Hick believed that after death there would be future lives, in this or other worlds, to enable the spiritual growth that would result in eternity with God.
- He rejected the teaching relating to everlasting suffering in Jesus' parable of the sheep and the goats.

Assessments of Hick's views

His ideas have not been widely accepted for a number of reasons:

- His claim that apparent incompatibilities between religions are insignificant is not a valid one. The views and practices of some religious groups (e.g. of suicide cults or the Islamic State) seem totally incompatible with those of any mainstream religion or society.
- Christianity traditionally thinks in terms of life, death, judgement and final state. Hick's idea of future states of existence after death does not fit in with this, so many Christians would reject it. The concept of **universalism** is unacceptable to evangelical Protestants, though acceptable to some liberal Protestants.
- Most religions reject the view that religion is about self-transformation rather than the quest for truth.

Hick's ideas do, however, go some way to promoting interfaith and interdenominational relations.

- His views about the cultural links between individuals and their religion encourage people to think about the one-ness of human religious understanding and not just about the differences between religions.
- His views on the nature of religion and on universalism could strengthen **interfaith** and **interdenominational relations**.

> ## Now test yourself
>
> 1 What view forms Hick's starting point on pluralism?
> 2 How, in Hick's view, has the relationship between humans and God been shaped?
> 3 What, according to Hick, is religion about?
> 4 Give one reason why most Christians have rejected Hick's approach.
> 5 What is meant by the term 'interfaith relations'?
>
> TESTED

Christian responses to issues of freedom of religious expression in society

Freedom of religious expression

As with adherents to other faiths, Christians have been given the right to express their religious beliefs and views in British society.

It is not an absolute right. If it would be harmful to others, would cause a breach of the peace or express racial or religious hatred that would be a breach of the law.

Christians may express their religious beliefs in a number of ways, but there may be a problem when the right to express religious beliefs or views clashes with other legislation. This has been demonstrated in the UK in a number of recent court cases.

Form of expression	Argument for right to religious expression	Argument against right to religious expression	Legal decision
Nada Eweida: Wearing a lapel cross on British Airways uniform	This expression of her faith would cause no harm.	Displays of religious affiliation inappropriate in workplace	For Nada Eweida Not restricting anyone else's rights
Shirley Chaplin: A nurse wearing a cross for work	This expression of her faith would cause no harm.	Prohibited by her NHS trust, so in breach of its rules	Against Shirley Chaplin Wearing any necklace a health risk in hospital
Mr and Mrs Bull refused a room at their guesthouse to a gay couple	The owners let rooms to married couples only; upholding Christian teaching on sexual practice. This was not a decision based on sexual orientation.	An act of discrimination on sexual orientation grounds	Against Mr and Mrs Bull Their action seen as a breach of the 2007 Sexual Orientation regulations
Margaret Jones, a registrar, said she could not conduct same-sex weddings	Expression of her Christian beliefs about marriage did not affect any couples. She was willing to register the marriage, simply leaving the other person on duty to perform the ceremony.	Conducting a ceremony did not prevent the *essential feature* of her faith: her right to worship as she wished	For Margaret Jones Council had not investigated ways of accommodating her concerns (she had been dismissed for gross misconduct)

Some key questions affect how these decisions were made.

- What is and is not an essential expression of faith?
- Should religion be a personal matter or should it be upheld by public institutions?
- How can society resolve the tensions between people's legal right to be treated with equal respect under the 2010 Act and the legal right of Christians to freedom of religious expression?

Now test yourself

1 What is meant by freedom of religious expression?
2 Give one reason why the right to freedom of religious expression is not an absolute right.
3 Why did the court find in favour of Nada Eweida's right to wear a cross on her BA uniform?
4 Why was a different decision made when a nurse claimed the right to wear a cross for work?
5 Why did the court state that Mr and Mrs Bull's refusal to accommodate a gay couple in their guesthouse was illegal?

Exam practice: A-level

1 a Examine why there are different Christian beliefs about the relationship between Christianity and other faiths.   [10 marks]
  b 'Karl Rahner's concept of 'anonymous Christians' is paternalistic.' Evaluate this claim.   [15 marks]
2 a Examine John Hick's pluralist understanding of religion.   [10 marks]
  b 'John Hick's views contradict key Christian beliefs.' Evaluate this claim.   [15 marks]
3 a Examine Christian responses to issues of freedom of expression.   [10 marks]
  b 'A person's right to freedom of religious expression should be absolute.'
    Evaluate this claim.   [15 marks]

10 Introduction to Dialogues

Dialogues questions

In Sections B and C of the Christianity Component, you are required to answer two questions that are referred to as Dialogues questions:
- One on the dialogue between Christianity and philosophy (section B)
- One on the dialogue between Christianity and ethics (section C).

The allocation of marks is exactly the same as for the other Component 1 and 2 questions:
- AO1 10 marks
- AO2 15 marks.

There are, however, significant differences between these questions and the others. In the Dialogues questions:
- there is a choice of question:
  - You answer one out of two questions on the dialogue between Christianity and philosophy.
  - You answer one out of two questions on the dialogue between Christianity and ethics.
- the questions are not split into two parts. They are global 'unstructured' questions:

Statement
Critically examine and evaluate this view with reference to the dialogue between Christianity and Philosophy. [25 marks]
or
Critically examine and evaluate this view with reference to the dialogue between Christianity and Ethics. [25 marks]
Or
Critically examine and evaluate this view with reference to the dialogue between Christianity and the views of a named school of thought/a named scholar. [25 marks]

- You are free to structure your answers as you wish.
  - You can separate the AO1 from the AO2 or you can combine them.
  - In the mark schemes, AO1 and AO2 are given separately, but that is for the convenience of examiners and others who study the mark schemes – for example, you and your teacher.

Preparing for Dialogues questions

You will not have much new content to learn; covering the Dialogues content is essentially revision of Components 1 and 2.

You need to make links between your areas of study.
- In answering a question, for example, about whether or not belief in God is reasonable, you need to include material that you have studied in both Components 1 and 2.
- What you select and how many topics you include is entirely your choice.
- The balance between Christianity and philosophy/ethics is also entirely your choice.
- As long as the material is relevant, it can come from any part of the material you have studied. For instance, in a question about whether belief in God is reasonable, you might wish to consider the problem of evil, and for this you could include material from both philosophy and ethics.

Lots of practice in writing this style of essay is very important.
- There are specimen and additional specimen questions with mark schemes. These give guidance on the kind of question that could be asked on all the topics listed.

Things to remember when answering Dialogues questions

- Questions in this section of your exam are deliberately broad and cover a range of topics you have already studied in Components 1 and 2.
- You need to focus on critical analysis/critical awareness/critical evaluation. The emphasis is on 'dialogue' (critical discussion) and not on giving lists of facts or lists of the views of different scholars, Christian denominations, etc.
  - Do not include too many topics, as your answer might become like a list of facts, losing the critical analysis.
  - AO2 is worth 60 per cent of the marks, so beware of giving lots of facts with little assessment.
- It is entirely up to you which topics you decide to include in your answer, but you must include a topic from each area of study. The balance between the two areas of study is entirely up to you.
- You do not need to go beyond the specification content for either the topic material itself or naming scholars. You may go beyond if you wish, but you will not lose marks by sticking to what is set in the specification.
- The questions set may not necessarily be concerned with Christianity against philosophy. Many philosophers were and are Christians and in some cases they have raised the issue being debated.
- Your answer need not be restricted to the debates that scholars conduct among themselves. You can engage in the dialogue with Christians and/or with scholars.
- The nature of the question is global, i.e. it is not separated out into two parts with one part for AO1 and one for AO2. You can structure your answer either:
  - globally, i.e. incorporating AO1 and AO2 in each of your paragraphs.
  - treating AO1 and AO2 separately, as with the non-dialogue questions.
- Allow about 45 minutes for planning and writing each answer: 18 minutes for AO1 and 27 minutes for AO2.

11 The dialogue between Christianity and philosophy

There are seven dialogue areas:
- God
- Self, death and afterlife
- Sources of wisdom and authority
- Religious experience
- The relationship between scientific and religious discourses
- The truth claims of other religions
- Miracles.

In each of these areas, this revision guide includes a table to show suggested links between Christianity, philosophy and named scholars. This should help you to structure your revision of those topics and think through how you could combine the topics in answering an exam question.

Two exam practice questions are given in each section to help you consider the key questions which you should address in all areas:
- How far is the belief reasonable?
  - Is it based on reason?
  - Is it consistent with reason?
- How meaningful are the statements of faith?
  - For whom are they meaningful?
- How coherent are the beliefs?
  - How consistent are they with other beliefs in the belief system?
- How relevant is philosophical enquiry for religious faith?
  - What is the importance of the distinction between 'belief in' and 'belief that'?

Before attempting a question, use the table to help you choose those topic areas that you feel most confident and comfortable with, in order to answer it. Make sure that you:
- include both Christianity and philosophy in your selection
- don't choose too many topics.

God

REVISED

Christianity

- Sources of wisdom and authority.
- God.
- Christianity and science (Darwin, Polkinghorne).
- Christianity and secularisation (McGrath, Dawkins).

Philosophy

Philosophy	Scholars
Arguments for existence of God	Paley/Anselm/Aquinas/Hume/Gaunilo/Kant/Russell
Evil and suffering	Hick/Griffin
Religious experience	Otto/James/Stace
Religious language	Hick/Hare/Wittgenstein/Tillich/Aquinas
Miracles	Hume/Wiles

Now test yourself answers at www.hoddereducation.co.uk/myrevisionnotes

Exam practice

'The Bible is unreliable as a source of authority for Christian understanding of God.' Critically examine and evaluate this view with reference to the dialogue between Christianity and philosophy.

[25 marks]

'Belief in God is reasonable.' Critically examine and evaluate this view with reference to the dialogue between Christianity and philosophy.

[25 marks]

Self, death and afterlife

REVISED

Christianity

- Sources of wisdom and authority
- Self, death and afterlife
- Good conduct and key moral principles
- Christianity, migration and religious pluralism (Hick)

Philosophy

Philosophy	Scholars
Religious language	Hick/Hare/Wittgenstein/Tillich/Aquinas
Self, death and the afterlife	Descartes

Exam practice

'Any talk of life after death is meaningless.' Critically examine and evaluate this view with reference to the dialogue between Christianity and philosophy. [25 marks]

'It is reasonable to believe in the resurrection of the body.' Critically examine and evaluate this view with reference to the dialogue between Christianity and philosophy. [25 marks]

Sources of wisdom and authority

Christianity

- Sources of wisdom and authority
- God
- Good conduct and key moral principles
- Expressions of religious identity
- Christianity, gender and sexuality
- Christianity and science (Darwin, Polkinghorne)
- Christianity and secularisation (McGrath, Dawkins)
- Christianity, migration and religious pluralism (Hick)

Philosophy

Philosophy	Scholars
Arguments for existence of God	Paley/Anselm/Aquinas/Hume/Gaunilo/Kant/Russell
Evil and suffering	Hick/Griffin
Religious experience	Otto/James/Stace
Religious language	Hick/Hare/Wittgenstein/Tillich/Aquinas
Miracles	Hume/Wiles

Exam practice

'Claims that any human source of authority is infallible are incoherent.' Critically examine and evaluate this view with reference to the dialogue between Christianity and philosophy. [25 marks]

'The arguments of militant atheism carry far more weight than any arguments for theism.' Critically examine and evaluate this view with reference to the dialogue between Christianity and philosophy.
[25 marks]

Religious experience

REVISED

Christianity

- Sources of wisdom and authority
- God
- Expressions of religious identity

Philosophy

Philosophy	Scholars
Religious experience	Otto/James/Stace
Religious language	Hick/Hare/Wittgenstein/Tillich/Aquinas
Miracles	Hume/Wiles

Exam practice

'Religious experience gives the best insights into the nature of God.' Critically examine and evaluate this view with reference to the dialogue between Christianity and philosophy. [25 marks]

'Religious experiences are meaningless.' Critically examine and evaluate this view with reference to the dialogue between Christianity and William James. [25 marks]

The relationship between scientific and religious discourses

REVISED

Christianity

- God
- Good conduct and key moral principles
- Christianity and science (Darwin, Polkinghorne)

Philosophy

Philosophy	Scholars
Arguments for existence of God	Paley/Anselm/Aquinas/Hume/Gaunilo/Kant/Russell
Religious experience	Otto/James/Stace
Religious language	Hick/Hare/Wittgenstein/Tillich/Aquinas
Miracles	Hume/Wiles
Self, death and the afterlife	Descartes

Exam practice

'Philosophical arguments relating to the existence of God are irrelevant to belief in God.' Critically examine and evaluate this view with reference to the dialogue between Christianity and philosophy. [25 marks]

'Christian arguments that oppose human genetic engineering are inconsistent with Christian beliefs about the value of human life.' Critically examine and evaluate this view with reference to the dialogue between Christianity and philosophy. [25 marks]

The truth claims of other religions

Christianity

- Sources of wisdom and authority
- God
- Expressions of religious identity
- Christianity, migration and religious pluralism (Hick)

Philosophy

Philosophy	Scholars
Religious experience	Otto/James/Stace
Religious language	Hick/Hare/Wittgenstein/Tillich/Aquinas
Miracles	Hume/Wiles
Self, death and the afterlife	Descartes

Exam practice

'Inclusivism is the only reasonable approach for Christians to take in multicultural Britain.' Critically examine and evaluate this view with reference to the dialogue between Christianity and philosophy.

[25 marks]

'The claims about God that are made in different religions are all equally valid.' Critically examine and evaluate this view with reference to the dialogue between Christianity and philosophy.

[25 marks]

Miracles

Christianity

- Sources of wisdom and authority
- God
- Christianity and science (Darwin, Polkinghorne)

Philosophy

Philosophy	Scholars
Evil and suffering	Hick/Griffin
Religious experience	Otto/James/Stace
Religious language	Hick/Hare/Wittgenstein/Tillich/Aquinas
Miracles	Hume/Wiles

Exam practice

'Belief in miracles is not consistent with belief in a God who loves all equally.' Critically examine and evaluate this view with reference to the dialogue between Christianity and philosophy.   [25 marks]

'Human experience shows that it is not reasonable to believe in the miracles recorded in the Bible.' Critically examine and evaluate this view with reference to the dialogue between Christianity and David Hume.   [25 marks]

12 The dialogue between ethics and Christianity

Christian responses to three approaches to moral decision-making

This area of the dialogue consists of ethical theory and applied ethics.

Illustration from applied ethics of the views of the three types of ethical theory and of Christian responses to them should come chiefly from the material in Chapter 4 of this revision guide and in particular:
- the 'strong' and 'weak' forms of the Sanctity of Life principle
- issues of dominion and stewardship over animals and the environment as a whole.

You could also refer to the other key principles:
- the four 'cardinal' virtues of prudence (practical wisdom), justice, fortitude (courage) and temperance (self-control)
- the three theological virtues of faith, hope and love.

Christian ethics as following ethical theory

REVISED

The extent to which Christian ethics can be categorised as one of the following three types of ethical theory is debated. The three types of ethical theory are:
- deontological ethics, with reference to Kant
- teleological and consequential ethics, with reference to Bentham
- character-based, with reference to Virtue Ethics.

Christianity will also be viewed from the perspectives of natural moral law theory (NML), divine command theory and Fletcher's situation ethics.

As you work through each type, consider:
- how far Christian ethics might be considered to be deontological, teleological or character-based
- the extent to which Christian ethics is compatible with the ethical theories of Bentham, Kant and Aristotle.

Ethics, with reference to Kant

Deontological ethics refers to morality based upon the idea of an intrinsic and objective right and wrong, and the resulting duty to do right. There are a number of views as to how the intrinsic points of right and wrong should be defined. You will need to be able to compare and contrast the views of Kant, natural moral law and divine command theory.

	Kant	Natural moral law	Divine command theory
Basis of deontology	Rule-based morality derived from rational assessment of our duty. Once we know through application of reason what our duty is, there is no need for any consideration of consequences. Doing right is nothing to do with obeying God-given rules, but is demanded by our nature as rational beings.	Rule-based morality discovered through human reason. Independent of special revelation as found in the Bible; laws found in the Bible are simply there as a reminder. Primary precepts are absolute and universal. Secondary precepts are in most cases absolute, though Aquinas allowed some flexibility in exceptional circumstances.	Obedience to God's laws as set out in scripture. Absolutely binding for all time as they are the infallible word of God.
Application of ethic	Application of three formulations of Categorical Imperative to tell us what is our duty: ● Universalisability ● Treating others as an end and not solely as a means ● Acting as law-making member of kingdom of ends.	Application of primary and secondary precepts, supported by teachings of the Bible and the *Magisterium* and the cardinal and theological virtues as set out by Aquinas.	Application of teachings found in the Bible as guided by the Holy Spirit in prayer.

Exam practice

'Kant's ethical theory is almost identical to Christian ethics.' Critically examine and evaluate this view with reference to the dialogue between Christianity and ethical studies.   [25 marks]

Now test yourself answers at **www.hoddereducation.co.uk/myrevisionnotes**

Teleological and consequentialist ethics, with reference to Bentham

Teleological and consequentialist ethics refer to morality based upon judging the consequences of one's actions, and acting so as to achieve a desired *telos* (goal). There are a number of views as to what this *telos* is, and therefore how the consequence of any choice or action should be assessed. You will need to be able to compare and contrast the views of Bentham, natural moral law, divine command theory and situation ethics.

	Bentham	Natural moral law	Divine command theory	Situation ethics
Basis of *telos*	*Telos* expressed in the Greatest Happiness Principle. *Telos* is to be experienced in this life as Bentham did not believe in life after death. Kant thought *telos* to be achievement of the *summum bonum*; the state where virtue is rewarded with happiness. In contrast to Bentham's view, this given by God after death.	Two aspects to *telos*: ● For humans as individuals, happiness in sense of 'human flourishing' on earth ● For humanity as a whole, the final *telos* is eternal joy after death through union with God.	*Telos* is heaven: the reward for a life lived for Christ, in obedience to Bible teachings.	For some, *telos* means the experience of *agape* for all in this world. For others, *telos* extends beyond death for the ultimate experience of *agape* in the presence of God.
Application of ethic	Act utilitarianism: the application of hedonic calculus to work out consequences in each situation. Consequences all-important.	Not a consequentialist approach. The emphasis is on absolute principles, rules and having the right intention rather than on consequences. Nevertheless, some aspects of natural moral law are teleological, particularly the primary precepts, which are concerned with the final end of humanity.	Not a consequentialist approach. The emphasis is on obedience to biblical commands, whatever the consequences.	Consequences are very important in working out what will affirm *agape* in each situation. It requires the application of the agapeic calculus to work out consequences in each situation. Essentially utilitarian.

Exam practice

'Christian ethics is teleological.' Critically examine and evaluate this view with reference to the dialogue between Christianity and ethical studies.

[25 marks]

Character-based ethics, with reference to Virtue Ethics

Character-based ethics refers to a morality that focuses primarily on what kind of person the individual should be rather than on the action that the individual should take. A good person will perform good actions. This type of ethics is known as Virtue Ethics. There are various forms of it, depending on which virtues are seen as important for the formation of a good character. You will need to be able to compare and contrast the views of Aristotle, natural moral law, divine command theory and situation ethics.

	Aristotle	Natural moral law	Divine command theory	Situation ethics
Basis of ethic	Agent-centred morality. A good action is one that arises out of the character of the agent. Humans are rational creatures, so the good life is one in which people reason well. Reasoning well means exercising virtue (moral excellence). The final *telos* of *eudaimonia* is achieved by being a virtuous person.	Aquinas combined aspects of Aristotle's Virtue Ethics with Christian ethics. Alongside his teaching on obedience to the primary and secondary precepts, he also emphasised four cardinal virtues taken from Aristotle's list and seen as attainable by human ability (prudence, justice, fortitude and self-control) + three theological virtues taken from 1 Corinthians 13 (faith, hope and love) which humans exercise through God's grace.	Obedience to the infallible word of God as set out in scripture entails above all following the teachings of Jesus as recorded in the Gospels. Jesus' focus was more on inner attitudes than on actions, and this can be seen especially in the Beatitudes (Matthew 5:1–12). Paul also emphasised the importance of transformation of the mind in Romans 12:2.	Fulfilling the principle of *agape* achieved by doing what will most affirm love in each situation. The six fundamental principles of situation ethics centre around the concept of *agape*. The fourth of these states that *agape* is not an emotion but an act of the will: it wills the neighbour's good, irrespective of liking. In a sense, *agape* is here akin to a virtue. It is an attitude that is then expressed in action. For Fletcher, motive is important.

	Aristotle	Natural moral law	Divine command theory	Situation ethics
Application of ethic	Someone becomes a virtuous person by practising virtues and by imitating virtuous people. For an action to be virtuous, the individual must act through knowledge of a situation and through rational choice rather than out of desire, wish or opinion. Certain virtues lie in the mean between two extremes; the virtues themselves do not change as qualities but the 'location' of the mean is relative to the individual's natural character in particular situations.	Aquinas distinguished between apparent and real goods. He claimed that sin arose out of people confusing the two. Developing the virtues through observing and imitating the actions of virtuous people enables an individual to pursue the real good. A good person is one who has a good character and this is attained through practice of the virtues as a way of life.	In the Sermon on the Mount (Matthew 5), Jesus taught that attitudes of anger and lust were as subject to God's judgement as the actions of murder and adultery that stemmed from them. He said that in order to reflect the nature of God in their lives, his followers should develop and practise the quality of unconditional love for all.	There are seven criteria to be considered, one of which is motive. But unlike Virtue Ethics, any rule might be broken if it led to the most *agape*. Aristotle stated explicitly that certain actions could never be virtuous.

Exam practice

'Situation ethics has nothing in common with virtue ethics.' Critically examine and evaluate this view with reference to the dialogue between Christianity and ethical studies.   [25 marks]

Christian responses to specific ethical issues

In examining Christian responses to these issues and those in the next two main sections, assess

- the extent to which they are compatible with one another
- the strengths and weaknesses of these views.

Issues of human life and death

REVISED

Issue	Natural moral law	Situation ethics
Embryo research	Tantamount to murder (breaking the sixth (fifth) commandment) as embryos are destroyed: the right to life begins from conception. Against primary precepts of reproduction, living in ordered society, worship of God (who is the creator of life). 'I knew you before you were born' (Jeremiah 1:5) is seen as teaching that God knows each human before birth, and as therefore supporting the idea of the embryo as a person right from conception.	Embryos are not persons so do not have rights. The good for actual persons is more important than for potential persons. With adequate controls in place, research is acceptable, since it may cure disease.
Cloning	Tantamount to murder (breaking the sixth (fifth) commandment) as embryos are destroyed: the right to life begins from conception. It is against the primary precepts of reproduction, living in ordered society, worship of God (who is the creator of life). Scripture teaches that God knew you before you were born (Jeremiah 1:5). It is seen as attempting to usurp God's role as creator. The good intention of developing effective medical treatments for currently incurable conditions through stem cell cloning does not neutralise a bad act.	Embryos are not persons so do not have rights. The good for actual persons is more important than for potential persons. With adequate controls in place, research is acceptable, since it may cure disease. It might be needed in future to enable survival in space if Earth becomes overcrowded.
'Designer' babies	Tantamount to murder (breaking the sixth (fifth) commandment) as embryos are destroyed: the right to life begins from conception. Against primary precepts of reproduction, living in ordered society, worship of God (who is the creator of life). Scripture teaches that God knew you before you were born (Jeremiah 1:5). It is seen as attempting to usurp God's role as creator. The good intention of using saviour sibling technology to save a sick child's life does not neutralise a bad act.	Embryos are not persons so do not have rights. The good for actual persons is more important than for potential persons. With adequate controls in place, research is acceptable, since it may cure disease, and improve the human race.

Now test yourself answers at **www.hoddereducation.co.uk/myrevisionnotes**

Issue	Natural moral law	Situation ethics
Abortion	Against the primary precepts of preservation of (innocent) life and of reproduction. Tantamount to murder (breaking the sixth (fifth) commandment). Indirect abortion permitted through principle of double effect. Strong Sanctity of Life principle.	Embryos are not persons so do not have rights. The good for actual persons is more important than for potential persons. Rightness/wrongness entirely situational. Quality of life is more important than sanctity of life. Rejection of casuistry in favour of agapeic calculus.
Euthanasia and assisted suicide	Aquinas says that suicide is against natural inclination to stay alive. Against primary precepts of preservation of (innocent) life and living in an ordered society. Allowing euthanasia ignores the value of suffering. Strong Sanctity of Life principle. Doctrine of ordinary/extraordinary means allows nature to take its course.	Fletcher was the president of the Euthanasia Society of America, in support of the right to die. Personality is sacred but mere existence is not. Quality of life is more important than sanctity of life. Use of agapeic calculus in assessing risks and what is most loving in each situation.
Capital punishment	Aquinas says that since it is lawful to kill a dangerous animal, the same applies to a dangerous (human) evil-doer. An executioner is not a murderer as this is the lawful taking of life. Permissible for deterrence, protection and retribution. Scripture supports capital punishment, with *Lex talionis* in Old Testament. The view of the Catechism of the Catholic Church (CCC) is that cases where there is an absolute necessity for the death penalty are very rare, if not practically non-existent.	No set view. Application of working principles is needed to decide what would be most loving in each situation for society as well as the individual.

Exam practice

'The creation of designer babies goes against Christian views on the value of human life.' Critically examine and evaluate this view with reference to the dialogue between Christianity and situation ethics.

[25 marks]

Issues of animal life and death

Issue	Natural moral law	Situation ethics
Use of animals as food; intensive farming	Animals are irrational and created for human use. Aquinas' opposition to cruelty would be against intensive farming.	Some would argue for extension of *agape* to animals, but most put human interests first. The human digestive system is adapted to meat-eating. Some would justify increase in intensive farming to address global hunger. Others might see reduction in animal farming would be more effective solution.
Use of animals in scientific procedures; cloning	Acceptable if animals are property. CCC: animal testing is permissible 'within reasonable limits'. Aquinas might have opposed cloning because it changes nature of a species; God created each to serve its purpose. Catholic Church accepts cloning to improve food production.	Fletcher was involved in cloning research and supported animal testing to promote human welfare and save human lives. Individuals to make up their own minds on this, but in general, the end justifies the means.
Blood sports	Acceptable if animals are property. But cruelty to animals could encourage cruelty to humans. CCC: humans owe animals kindness. CCC: 'Contrary to human dignity to cause animals to suffer or die needlessly'.	Nothing agapeic about blood sports. Most would not put human pleasure before something that caused terrible suffering. Watching blood sports desensitises people to violence, so is not loving. Some might argue that fox-hunting is agapeic because of the damage done by foxes.
Animals as a source of organs for transplants	Acceptable as long as it does not affect the human germline. Acceptable as long as pain relieved and suffering minimised.	Situation ethics directed at persons so it depends on status of animals. Would address shortage of organs and benefit those in need. Agapeic calculus needed to take risks into account.

Exam practice

'The use of animals in scientific procedures is incompatible with Christian compassion.' Critically examine and evaluate this view with reference to the dialogue between Christianity and ethical studies.

[25 marks]

Theft and lying

Issue	Natural moral law	Situation ethics
Theft	Against primary precept of living in ordered society. Against the eighth (seventh) commandment: You shall not steal. Aquinas says it may be permissible under the law of double effect, for example, if a starving man stole from a rich man or if someone stole to save someone from starvation.	Rightness/wrongness not decided by casuistry but by the situation: ● Does it show love of neighbour? ● Does it lead to justice?
Lying	Against primary precept of living in ordered society. Against the ninth (eighth) commandment: You shall not bear false witness against your neighbour. Never permissible, even to save a life, but hiding the truth may be acceptable.	No intrinsic right/wrong. Depends on what is the most loving in each situation.

Exam practice

'For both Christianity and Virtue Ethics, telling lies is wrong.' Critically examine and evaluate this view with reference to the dialogue between Christianity and ethical studies. [25 marks]

Homosexuality and transgender issues

Issue	Evangelical Protestants	Catholics	Liberal Protestants
Homosexuality	Declared 'an abomination' in the Bible. Both orientation and practice are sinful. There could be encouragement of medical and psychological treatment to change a person's orientation.	Distinction between orientation and practice: orientation not sinful, but practice is against primary precept of reproduction. Gay people to be shown respect and acceptance.	Biblical denunciations seen as product of their time. Full acceptance of gay people as Church members and clergy.
Transgender	God decides a person's gender; to seek to change it is an act of rebellion against God.	Against changing gender: surgery does not change identity. Possibly permissible in extreme cases but wholesale acceptance could lead to humankind's self-destruction. Marriage of transgender individuals is not permitted.	Acceptance of transgender people and rights. Acceptance as members of the Church and as clergy. Marriage is permitted.

Exam practice

'Modern ethical theories are more helpful than Aquinas' natural moral law theory in addressing the issue of homosexuality.' Critically examine and evaluate this view with reference to the dialogue between Christianity and ethical studies. [25 marks]

Marriage and divorce

REVISED

Issue	Evangelical Protestants	Catholics	Liberal Protestants
Marriage and divorce	A husband is to be obeyed by his wife. Procreation an important part of marriage, as it fulfils the command in Genesis 1. Divorce only permitted on the grounds of adultery. Remarriage is not biblical.	Marriage is a sacrament and a partnership. Procreation is a primary purpose of sex though not the only purpose. Marriage is for life. Divorce is recognised, but there can be no remarriage without an annulment.	Marriage is an ordinance and a partnership. Sex is more about enriching relationships than about procreation. The ideal is marriage for life, but there is an acceptance of divorce and remarriage.

Exam practice

'Remarriage after divorce undermines Christian beliefs about marriage.' Critically examine and evaluate this view with reference to the dialogue between Christianity and ethical studies.   [25 marks]

Genetic engineering

REVISED

Mainstream denominations	Situation ethics
Crops There are concerns about environmental effects, but acknowledgement that the practice could reduce world hunger. **Animals** Some support practice as way of boosting food production, but not to be done for trivial reasons, or if it would cause animal suffering. Concern about transmission of animal diseases with xenotransplantation. **Humans** Human somatic-cell therapy acceptable as an act of compassion when the benefits outweigh the risks and costs. Germline therapy raises concerns about safety and possibility of unwanted, harmful effects on future generations. Against enhancement therapy as idolatrous, and risking promotion of a two-tier society.	Need for proper controls to prevent abuse and exploitation, but acceptance of all forms as in human interests. Rejection of traditional Christian views as outdated and irrelevant. Supports enhancement therapy as way of improving human species and possibly meeting future need for living in totally different environment from Earth.

Exam practice

'Christian views on human genetic engineering are incompatible with those of secular ethics.' Critically examine and evaluate this view with reference to the dialogue between Christianity and ethical studies.

[25 marks]

Christian responses to issues surrounding wealth, tolerance and freedom of expression

Wealth

REVISED

New Testament	Mainstream denominations	Bruderhof
Story of Zacchaeus suggests Jesus did not see wealth as wrong in itself, but saw it as potentially a great hindrance in spiritual life. Attitude to possessions is all-important, and in some cases, sacrifice of possessions necessary. Early Church in Jerusalem shared everything, showing the importance of generosity. Wealth is morally neutral but can interfere with relationship with God: the possessor's attitude is key.	Some Pentecostals accept prosperity theology: wealth is God's reward for faith and obedience to his laws. Most Christians believe wealth is not wrong in itself, but it brings the responsibility to share with those in need, and be a good steward. Catholic and Anglican monastics take vow of poverty as sign of total devotion to God.	Materialism one of the chief causes of the ills of modern society. Members of the community have no personal property and take vow to live simply.

Exam practice

'For Christians, being wealthy is wrong.' Critically examine and evaluate this view with reference to the dialogue between Christianity and ethical studies. [25 marks]

Tolerance and freedom of religious expression

REVISED

	Mainstream denominations	Evangelical Protestants
Tolerance	An inclusivist attitude to one another and to non-Christians promotes respect for all. A spirit of tolerance is a directing force within ecumenism. Catholicism tends to reflect closed inclusivism.	An exclusivist attitude is held toward all who do not accept a fundamentalist approach to the teachings of the Bible. Salvation is through faith in Jesus as saviour alone, and shown by obedience to God's word.
Freedom of religious expression	Freedom of religious expression is promoted. The duty to protest against what is seen as morally wrong is upheld, but should be expressed with love and in sensitivity to others' views. There is acceptance of limits to freedom where it would harm others or be inflammatory. Against the use of violence.	Freedom of religious expression is promoted. Active evangelism is important, to lead to salvation of as many people as possible. The duty to protest against what is seen as morally wrong is upheld, and might occasionally include verbal or even physical opposition to those with different views, e.g. at abortion clinics.

Exam practice

'In opposing great moral evils, Christians might be justified in using violent protest.' Critically examine and evaluate this view with reference to the dialogue between Christianity and ethical studies.
[25 marks]

Christian understandings of free will and moral responsibility, and the value of conscience

Christian understandings of free will and moral responsibility

	Christian determinism	Non-determinist Christian views
Free will	God's omnipotence means he controls everything, including human decision-making. God's omniscience is causative, so his prior knowledge of human decisions is their cause. Belief in predestination based on Paul's letter to Christians in Rome. Calvin's view that some are eternally chosen for joys of heaven and others for torments of hell.	Free will is one of God's most precious gifts to humanity – God does not override it. Voluntarily restricts omnipotence to allow for human moral freedom. Omniscience not causative: Aquinas: God does not exist in time; seeing results of future free choices does not mean he causes them. Process theology: God exists in time so cannot know the future.
Moral responsibility	Humans are still morally responsible for their actions. Calvin: humans don't know what God has decided.	Three aspects to moral responsibility: ● No responsibility when decision out of our control. ● Diminished responsibility when an overwhelmingly strong influence affects/restricts our freedom of choice. ● Full responsibility when our decisions are knowingly and freely made.

Exam practice

'Hard determinism provides an effective challenge to Christian understandings of free will.' Critically examine and evaluate this view with reference to the dialogue between Christianity and ethical studies.

[25 marks]

The value of conscience in Christian moral decision-making

Conscience is the inner conviction that a thought or action is right or wrong. Most people seem to experience it, often in the form of feeling guilty or ashamed. There are many different views about its nature and origin.

	Augustine	Aquinas	Butler	Fletcher
Nature	Augustine: the voice of God whispering to us. Direct revelation from God.	'The mind of man making moral judgements'. An activity of reason. Entails knowledge of facts of a situation. Reflection on human nature leads to understanding of basic moral principles as revealed in natural moral law's primary precepts and Bible teachings. Conscience applies these principles to the situation.	God-given natural intuitive ability to reflect morally on past actions and what an individual is about to do. Performs a balancing role between two aspects of our nature: egoism and altruism. Balance needed in both personal life and as member of society.	Rejects traditional religious and secular views of conscience. Conscience is a verb, not a noun. It is not something we have, but something people do. It is a method of assessment, choosing what *agape* demands in each situation.
Value	Bonhoeffer thought that conscience must be obeyed even if it entails setting aside traditional moral principles.	Conscience must always be followed, even though it could be mistaken through inaccurate understanding of the situation, as human reason is not infallible. Fully informing the conscience through studying the teachings of the Bible and the Church, and through prayer and sacrament, is important to lessen the likelihood of it being mistaken.	Conscience must be obeyed since it is a God-given faculty. In most cases, humans would know intuitively what was right.	It is simply a description of the decision-making process so plays no important role in Fletcher's situation ethics.

Exam practice

'Traditional Christian views about conscience are invalidated by modern non-religious views.' Critically examine and evaluate this view with reference to the dialogue between Christianity and ethical studies.

[25 marks]

The impact of other ethical perspectives and ethical studies on Christian views about these issues

Challenges to and support for Christian views

	Bentham	Kant	Virtue ethics
Challenge	Rejection of religious basis and rule-based morality. Rejection of Sanctity of Life Principle in favour of quality of life. Regards traditional Christian views on animals as inhumane and wrong.	Rejects idea of God and the Bible as the source or basis of morality. Opposed to consequentialist and relativist ideas such as those of Fletcher.	Considers some of Jesus' teaching very extreme; for Aristotle, the doctrine of the mean was crucial. Fletcher's ethics allowed anything if it produced the most *agape*; this included actions that Aristotle claimed could never be virtuous.
Support	Like Christian Situation ethicists, Bentham has strong consequentialist ethic and is willing to set aside rules. Supports liberal Christian view of the importance of quality of life.	Supports views of natural moral law that forbid exploitation of humans as means to an end.	Jesus stressed the importance to morality of intention and the person's inner disposition. Aquinas highlighted the importance of four cardinal virtues taken from Aristotle. Some notable virtue ethicists are/were Christians.

There are many criticisms of Christian ethical teaching:
- The appeal made to ancient texts (natural moral law and divine command theory) and medieval thought (natural moral law) to justify views on essentially modern ethical issues.
- The vagueness of Fletcher's situation ethics as a moral guide.

You should consider the extent to which such criticisms are valid and if they are, whether they invalidate Christianity as a whole and its sources of authority.

Exam practice

'The authority of Christian statements on modern ethical issues is weakened by their reliance on teachings from the distant past.' Critically examine and evaluate this view with reference to the dialogue between Christianity and ethical studies.

[25 marks]

Notes

Now test yourself answers at www.hoddereducation.co.uk/myrevisionnotes